REGENTS RENAISSANCE DRAMA SERIES

General Editor: Cyrus Hoy
Advisory Editor: G. E. Bentley

THE DEVIL'S LAW-CASE

JOHN WEBSTER

The Devil's Law-Case

Edited by

FRANCES A. SHIRLEY

UNIVERSITY OF NEBRASKA PRESS · LINCOLN

Publishers on the Plains
UNP

International Standard Book Number 0–8032–0296–2
Library of Congress Catalog Card Number: ~~68–20771~~

MANUFACTURED IN THE UNITED STATES OF AMERICA

Regents Renaissance Drama Series

The purpose of the Regents Renaissance Drama Series is to provide soundly edited texts, in modern spelling, of the more significant plays of the Elizabethan, Jacobean, and Caroline theater. Each text in the series is based on a fresh collation of all sixteenth- and seventeenth-century editions. The textual notes, which appear above the line at the bottom of each page, record all substantive departures from the edition used as the copy-text. Variant substantive readings among sixteenth- and seventeenth-century editions are listed there as well. In cases where two or more of the old editions present widely divergent readings, a list of substantive variants in editions through the seventeenth century is given in an appendix. Editions after 1700 are referred to in the textual notes only when an emendation originating in some one of them is received into the text. Variants of accidentals (spelling, punctuation, capitalization) are not recorded in the notes. Contracted forms of characters' names are silently expanded in speech prefixes and stage directions, and, in the case of speech prefixes, are regularized. Additions to the stage directions of the copy-text are enclosed in brackets. Stage directions such as "within" or "aside" are enclosed in parentheses when they occur in the copy-text.

Spelling has been modernized along consciously conservative lines. "Murther" has become "murder," and "burthen," "burden," but within the limits of a modernized text, and with the following exceptions, the linguistic quality of the original has been carefully preserved. The variety of contracted forms (*'em*, *'am*, *'m*, *'um*, *'hem*) used in the drama of the period for the pronoun *them* are here regularly given as *'em*, and the alternation between *a'th'* and *o'th'* (for *on* or *of the*) is regularly reproduced as *o'th'*. The copy-text distinction between preterite endings in *-d* and *-ed* is preserved except where the elision of *e* occurs in the penultimate syllable; in such cases, the final syllable is contracted. Thus, where the old editions read "threat'ned," those of the present series read "threaten'd." Where, in the old editions, a contracted preterite in *-y'd* would yield *-i'd* in modern spelling (as in "try'd," "cry'd," "deny'd"), the word is here given in its full form (e.g., "tried," "cried," "denied").

Punctuation has been brought into accord with modern practices. The effort here has been to achieve a balance between the generally light pointing of the old editions, and a system of punctuation which, without overloading the text with exclamation marks, semicolons, and dashes, will make the often loosely flowing verse (and prose) of the original syntactically intelligible to the modern reader. Dashes are regularly used only to indicate interrupted speeches, or shifts of address within a single speech.

Explanatory notes, chiefly concerned with glossing obsolete words and phrases, are printed below the textual notes at the bottom of each page. References to stage directions in the notes follow the admirable system of the Revels editions, whereby stage directions are keyed, decimally, to the line of the text before or after which they occur. Thus, a note on 0.2 has reference to the second line of the stage direction at the beginning of the scene in question. A note on 115.1 has reference to the first line of the stage direction following line 115 of the text of the relevant scene.

CYRUS HOY

University of Rochester

Contents

List of Abbreviations

Arcadia	Sir Philip Sidney. *Arcadia*. Ed. A. Feuillerat. Cambridge, 1922.
corr.	corrected
Dyce	Alexander Dyce, ed. *The Works of John Webster*. Revised edn. London, 1857.
Easy	Benjamin Easy. "Webster's 'Devil's Law Case'; Its Date." *Notes and Queries*, Third Series, IV (Sept. 19, 1863), 225–226.
Florio	John Florio. *Vocabulario Italiano & inglese*. London, 1688.
Gerard	John Gerard. *The herball, or General historie of plantes*. London, 1636.
Hazlitt	William Hazlitt, ed. *The Dramatic Works of John Webster*. Vol. III. London, 1857.
Horace	Quintus Horatius Flaccus. *The Satires, Epistles, and Art of Poetry*. Ed. John Conington. London, 1880.
Lucas	F. L. Lucas, ed. *The Complete Works of John Webster*. Vol. II. London, 1927.
OED	*Oxford English Dictionary*
Q	Quarto of 1623
S.D.	stage direction
S.P.	speech prefix
Stoll	E. E. Stoll. *John Webster*. Boston, 1905.
Sykes	H. Dugdale Sykes. "Date of Webster's Play, 'The Devil's Law Case.'" *Notes and Queries*, Eleventh Series, VII (Feb. 8, 1913), 106–107.
Trevelyan	G. M. Trevelyan. *Illustrated English Social History*. Vol. II. London, 1951.
uncorr.	uncorrected

Introduction

DATE AND STAGE HISTORY

There was no equivalent of Henslowe's *Diary* to record the composition of the last play Webster wrote alone, nor is there any note of a license for performance or printing. Dating *The Devil's Law-Case* becomes, therefore, a matter of working backward from the year of publication, 1623, taking into account internal evidence and the clues given on the title page:

> The Deuils Law-case./ OR,/ When Women goe to Law, the/ Deuill is full of Businesse./ *A new Tragecomoedy./ The true and perfect Copie from the Originall.*/ As it was approouedly well Acted/ by her Maiesties Seruants./ *Written by* IOHN WEBSTER./ *Non quam diu, sed quam bene.*/ [ornament]/ LONDON,/ Printed by *A.M.* for *Iohn Grismand*, and are/ to be sold at his Shop in Pauls Alley at the/ Signe of the Gunne. 1623.

Unlike *The Duchess of Malfi*, probably written in 1612 or 1613 and printed a decade later, *The Devil's Law-Case* seems to have been published reasonably quickly. At least, the title page tells us it is "new" and Webster, in his letter of dedication to Sir Thomas Finch, implies that this play will be new to a man who has already seen some of his "other works, as *The White Devil, The Duchess of Malfi, Guise*, and others." The date of *Guise* is unknown, and a forged insertion in Henslowe's *Diary* for November, 1601, is no proof that "Gwisse" is early Webster. The consensus of critical postulation is that the lost *Guise* succeeded Webster's great tragedies, which would then push the date of *The Devil's Law-Case* up to 1615 or 1616. In fact, only Fleay and Professor Bentley suggest an earlier year. Fleay uses the figures given in the trial scene: the Crispiano affair was in 1571, Romelio would have been born in 1572, Romelio is now thirty-eight; therefore the play must take place in 1610, which would also be the date of composition.[1] Bentley concurs, stating that where dates

[1] F. G. Fleay, *A Biographical Chronicle of the English Drama, 1559–1642* (London, 1891), II, 272–273. Alfred Harbage, opining 1617, allows a range of 1610–1619 in the revised edition of *Annals of English Drama* (London, 1964).

are so carefully reiterated, the present time of the play coincides with that of the first audiences.[2] This seems a bit tenuous in view of other internal evidence, especially since the dates are being reiterated to trap Winifrid in a lie.

The title page does give more conclusive evidence for a terminal date. Queen Anne died in 1619, and "her Maiesties Seruants" began to scatter, although the remains of the company may have continued, informally at least, to use the old name until they disbanded in the summer of 1622. Stoll, Bourgeois, and Lucas feel that the play need not have been acted during Queen Anne's lifetime, but had to be on the boards before July 25, 1622.[3] It seems probable that in the years following Queen Anne's death, the company came to be thought of in connection with its theater, the Red Bull, and that the phrasing of the title page at least indicates a date closer to 1619 than to a later period.

Internal evidence is small help in narrowing the span of years, but it does make more certain a postulation of 1617–1621. Webster has a habit of echoing himself and others. Lines reminiscent of Sidney's *Arcadia* abound, as well as snatches from *The Duchess of Malfi* and *The White Devil*. These latter are occasionally better phrased than in the original, but frequently less organic to the passages where they occur, as if spatchcocked in where convenient. More germane to dating the play are lines pointed out by Dyce (I.ii.181–192)[4] and Sykes (II.i.161–164)[5] that parallel and even repeat phrases from Jonson's *The Devil is an Ass*, which was acted in 1616, although not printed until 1631.

A passing reference to some persons having recently been peppered in the East Indies (IV.ii.11–13) has provided yet another faint clue. Dyce assumed that Webster was referring to the Massacre of Amboyna, in February 1622/23,[6] but Sykes pointed out that the news reached England in 1624, after *The Devil's Law-Case* was in print.[7]

2 G. E. Bentley, *The Jacobean and Caroline Stage* (Oxford, 1956), V, 1251.

3 E. E. Stoll, *John Webster* (Boston, 1905), p. 32; A. F. Bourgeois, "John Webster: The Probable Date of 'The Devil's Law Case,'" *Notes and Queries*, Eleventh Series, X (July 18, 1914), 41; F. L. Lucas, ed., John Webster, *Works* (London, 1927), II, 213.

4 Alexander Dyce, ed., *The Works of John Webster* (London, 1857), p. 112.

5 H. Dugdale Sykes, "Date of Webster's Play, 'The Devil's Law Case,'" *Notes and Queries*, Eleventh Series, VII (Feb. 8, 1913), 106.

6 Dyce, *Works*, p. 131 n.

7 Sykes, "Date," p. 106.

It was Stoll who found a more likely incident: in 1619, English ships picking up pepper in Sumatra were attacked by a larger Dutch fleet, and the news soon reached England.[8] The specific cargo may well have suggested "peppered" to Webster, who delighted in word play. On the other hand, after April, 1618, encounters with the Dutch were frequent and Webster may have had no one incident in mind.

Lucas points out another apparently topical allusion: "there has been gold convey'd beyond the sea in hollow anchors" (II.i.208–209). Foreign merchants had been accused and tried for smuggling huge amounts of gold out of the country in 1619.[9] A contemporary audience would have thought of this, just as they would have run through the dates of great frosts and plagues during the trial scene. There was a severe freeze in 1621, as a matter of fact, and since Winifrid is trying to establish old age, she would have named three, not two great frosts in a play written after 1621.[10] The hunt for allusions gets on shakier ground as it proceeds. Is Webster thinking of Sir Richard Hawkins, who wrote in 1622, when he has Ariosto speak of the ominous names of ships (II.iii.58–67)?[11] The wording and names differ, however, and the idea is not unusual. Does Webster have in mind Henry Peachum's book, published in 1622, when he makes Romelio comment on becoming a "completer gentleman" (I.i.36)? Again, the concept is too general to support a 1622 date for Webster's play.

One final bit of investigation leads to the problem of sources, but never brings us to a date. It has been suggested that the trial and accusation of illegitimacy may have come from Fletcher and Massinger's *The Spanish Curate*, where an illegitimate child is acknowledged as part of a disinheritance plot, but this play seems to date from 1622 or later. *Lust's Dominion* comes closer in mood and motive, for there the child is claimed illegitimate from a desire for revenge; but the work is Elizabethan and does not help us here. Scholars have also noted early seventeenth-century trials that might have provided the incidents of the play.[12] One must always keep in mind, however,

[8] Stoll, *John Webster*, p. 31; Lucas, *Works*, II, 214.

[9] Lucas, *Works*, II, 216.

[10] Ibid., p. 214.

[11] Benjamin Easy, "Webster's 'Devil's Law Case'; Its Date," *Notes and Queries*, Third Series, IV (Sept. 19, 1863), 226.

[12] Lucas summarizes them in *Works*, II, 218–219. C. E. Vaughan calls attention to a French trial in 1610–1611, when an investigator had the name Romillon (*Cambridge History of English Literature* [New York, 1910], VI, 207).

that Webster's plays are full of legal terms, that other plays he was connected with have trial scenes (*The White Devil*, *Sir Thomas Wyatt*, *Appius and Virginia*, *The Fair Maid of the Inn*),[13] and that the forward behavior of the women seems more an amalgam of various ideas than a borrowing from a single dateable source.

Webster was not known as a speedy writer. He may well have begun *The Devil's Law-Case* in 1617 or 1618 and continued to tinker with it into 1619 or 1620, perhaps even making an addition or two before it was printed.[14] 1619 seems a reasonable choice of date, for the play would have been relatively new when printed, could have been on the boards while the players were thought of as the Queen's, and would have been contemporaneous with the few topical allusions it contains.

The Devil's Law-Case seems never to have been so popular as Webster's two masterpieces, despite the apocryphal "this is a good play, and met with success,"[15] and Thomas Hall's description of Webster as "that Poet whose glory was once to be the Author of Stage-plaies (as the Devils Law-case)."[16] There was no second edition in the seventeenth century, and there is no stage history since the Restoration. In fact, we have only the words of the title page and Webster's paragraph to the reader to indicate that it was ever performed. Despite this, Bentley is on relatively solid ground when he suggests that Richard Perkins played the part of Romelio.[17] Perkins was a respected actor with the Red Bull Company, and stuck with the troupe until it completely disbanded. He had won Webster's praise earlier for his part in *The White Devil*, was to be commended for his acting of Marlowe's Jew of Malta in revival, and probably could portray the mixture of brilliance and baseness the Webster role demands.

THE PLAY

One feels strangely disoriented while reading *The Devil's Law-Case*, partly because it is not what one expects of Webster, and partly

13 Except for the *White Devil*, of course, there is an authorship question for each of these.

14 Bourgeois suggests that the Contarino/Jolenta/Ercole/Romelio story was started before 1618, that Webster needed more material, and that a lawsuit suggested Leonora's scheme ("John Webster," p. 42).

15 D. E. Baker, I. Reed, and S. Jones, *Biographia Dramatica* (London, 1812), II, 160–161.

16 *Histrio-Mastix*, quoted in Dyce, *Works*, p. xix.

17 Bentley, *Jacobean and Caroline Stage*, V, 1251.

because of the play itself. There ought to be a more precise way of characterizing it than Fletcher's definition of tragicomedy: "It wants deaths, which is enough to make it no tragedy, yet brings some near it, which is enough to make it no comedy."[18] Although the juxtaposition of serious and comic can be the most effective way of making a point, Webster here seems unsure of his aim, or even as if he is forcing himself to work at variance with his native bent. He is attempting a form, popular in the Jacobean era, where chance, or a character functioning as a *deus ex machina*, saves people doomed to lose not only their loves, but also their lives. Although the form requires a darker sort of writing than comedy to make its threatening moments convincing, it also needs control of the shift to happier events. Webster's darker scenes are among his best, and Leonora's expression of grief and vow of vengeance begins as a poetic high point (III.iii. 257 ff.). It is in keeping with her earlier curse (I.ii.105–107), but as it becomes more melodramatic, it seems inappropriate to much of the play. Webster may be attempting mockery, of course, for Leonora's vow leads to a trial that becomes a travesty when it depends on the testimony of the shameless waiting-woman. On the other hand, he may be trying to show the extent of her passion as an excuse for her subsequent behavior.

Two later scenes, taken together, better illustrate the lack of precise control. The fourth scene of Act V is relatively long and opens with Julio's talk of the duel he does not wish to fight, and which we cannot take seriously. Characteristically, Webster pauses to tell a story, and a tenth of the scene is devoted to Julio's tale of a Welsh gentleman and toasted cheese. The mood shifts with the entrance of Romelio and the Capuchin. Romelio, believing himself guilty of murder, is about to undergo trial by combat; the friar, who knows of his accidental innocence, hopes for signs of penitence. Romelio brushes spiritual considerations aside, but exhibits a courage about fighting and death that the Capuchin cannot understand.

Suddenly, Leonora enters with a masque-like procession of coffins and winding sheets. Typically Websterian theatricality, and intended to bring home the horror of impending death, it seems to elicit proper sentiments from Romelio. He launches into a series of

[18] John Fletcher, "To the Reader," *The Faithful Shepherdess*, ed. W. W. Greg, *The Works of Francis Beaumont and John Fletcher* (London, 1908), III, 18.

sententious tetrameter couplets that are in sharp contrast to his more original, cynical meditation in II.iii:

> All the flowers of the spring
> Meet to perfume our burying:
> These have but their growing prime,
> And man does flourish but his time. . . .
> (V.iv.128 ff.)[19]

Caught off guard, we may be convinced of his change of heart, as Leonora and the Capuchin are. In a moment, however, he has tricked them into a tower, and we realize that the lines have been said with the same cynicism that characterizes much of the play.

The procession and the forty lines following it do serve several functions. Ironically, Romelio's cleverness delays the revelation that would save him from the combat. The macabre moment when Julio drapes himself in a shroud adds to the cynicism. The procession itself may have been intended to hammer home to the audience the stark reality of the impending combat, which on the surface will appear exciting and colorful. But in an overly crowded fifth act this seems an elaborate way to give one more twist to the story, and it detracts from the equally theatrical sixth scene with its lists and pageantry.

From the leisurely pace of the fourth scene, the reader is perfunctorily rushed through to the end as if Webster suddenly felt the play had become too long.[20] The fifth scene suffers in consequence. Leonora and the Capuchin are supposedly locked in a turret of Castel Nuovo, facing the sea where "not any creature can hear." Leonora, single-mindedly bent on stopping the combat, threatens to leap from the battlements. The Capuchin relies on Heaven's power, reminding her that Contarino has been miraculously saved, and insisting that the schemes of Romelio and other villains can never succeed:

> While they aspire to do themselves most right,
> The devil that rules i'th'air hangs in their light.
> (V.v.22–23)

19 Lucas comments on the inappropriateness of the speech on Romelio's lips, but sees the poetry in the man (*Works*, II, 361). There is a similar "meditation" in *Duchess of Malfi*, in the mouth of Bosola (II.i).

20 *The Devil's Law-Case* and *The White Devil* are the same length, *The Duchess of Malfi* a few hundred lines longer.

One of the most oppressive images in Stuart drama, and made more so by the change of "stands" to "hangs" in this play, the second line here might be Webster's own comment, whereas in *The Duchess of Malfi* (II.i.98) it seems more expressive of the mood of the play. But suddenly having a devil ruling in the air, even if only to affect sinners, seems at variance with the powerful Heaven of a few lines earlier, although Heaven does not obviously shape the end of *The Devil's Law-Case*. The scene closes abruptly and carelessly as Leonora breaks in with "ope the other casement/ That looks into the city"; the Capuchin answers simply, "Madam, I shall," and they leave.

The hasty juxtaposition of scenes, the quick shifts in fortune, the scramble to tie up loose ends and mete out rewards and punishments are characteristic of Jacobean and Caroline tragicomedies, and often give modern readers pause as they attempt to evaluate such plays. There is a mercurial, almost childish shifting of mood, and a belief that all can be made right, even to the final matchmaking that pairs Romelio and his nun. Most difficult for our psychologically oriented minds to grasp is the frequent lack of motivation. In *The Devil's Law-Case* there is much we must not question, such as Contarino's remaining in disguise (Lucas assumes it is because he likes to settle as much as possible in duels), or Jolenta's willingness to turn to Ercole.

It is easy to point to faults and lapses in this play, harder to explain the fascination of Romelio, and most difficult to see in the paradoxes some unifying pattern or point of view. Leech, in fact, puts the problem well as he speaks of Jacobean plays, where one is no longer sure which side to take, where the clear Elizabethan theses have vanished and the emphasis is on individual truths rather than general principles.[21]

Webster has created his own story, although turning to other works for occasional lines and in two instances borrowing an important event, the illegitimacy accusation and the fortuitous stabbing. As I noted earlier, several seventeenth-century plays contain similar charges of bastardy.[22] Stoll treats in some detail the other literary sources for Leonora's falsely labeling Romelio illegitimate at the expense of her own reputation. The earliest is Bernardo Giustiniani's

21 Clifford Leech, *John Webster: A Critical Study* (London, 1951), p. 59.

22 *The Spanish Curate* and *The Fair Maid of the Inn* are probably both too late; *Lust's Dominion* is not so close as the earlier non-dramatic parallels cited by Stoll, for it has no trial.

version in *De Origine Urbis Gestisque Venetorum* (1492), copied by Joannes Magnus in *De omnibus Gothorum Sueonumque Regibus* (1554). Stoll also cites a later version, less close to Webster's tale, in Nicolas Caussin's *Holy Court* (*Sainte Cour*). In all three, Theodoric is the wise judge who catches the mother in her lie as she tries to disinherit her son. In the earlier stories, furthermore, the widow has lived many years with her son and tries to turn him out at the behest of a lover. But as Stoll points out, this is the sort of popular tale that Webster might have picked up from another source.[23] Romelio's vengeful stabbing that accidentally saves the doomed Contarino has been traced to Goulart's *Histoires Admirables*, which had been translated into English by Grimeston by 1607.[24]

With one exception, other borrowings or parallels are relatively unimportant. Webster reworks lines from his two tragedies—in all three plays, for example, the glowworm becomes an image of the gap between appearance and reality.[25] He often echoes lines from other authors, a practice acceptable in the days of commonplace books. Critics have frequently pointed out the more important influence, not on lines, but on character, of Marlowe's *Jew of Malta*. We may list the numerous points of comparison; we must be sure to remember the divergences, for Romelio never becomes a caricature as does Barabas, and he retains our sympathy.

Both merchants have amassed great wealth and scorn lesser amounts; Romelio immediately shows contempt for Baptista who labors for "poor fifty thousand duckets."[26] Both, as Lucas notes, try to arrange a marriage and both cause rival suitors to duel, although Ercole and Contarino's fight results in a renewal of friendship rather than death.[27] Both men assume disguises when they attempt vengeful murder, Barabas becoming a French musician and Romelio dressing like a Jew. Romelio, in disguise, gives a catalogue of Italian Renaissance villainy surpassed only by Barabas and Ithamore's boasting

[23] Stoll, *John Webster*, pp. 156–158. He suggests that Dekker, et al., in *Lust's Dominion*, were using the same source, and Webster drew from that.

[24] Lucas, *Works*, II, 217. Langbaine first pointed out the source.

[25] *White Devil*, V.i.38 f.; *Duchess of Malfi*, IV.ii.141 f.; *Devil's Law-Case*, IV.ii.116 f. (Ingeborg Glier, *Struktur und Gestaltungsprinzipien in den Dramen John Websters* [Memmingen/Allgäu, 1957], p. 82).

[26] The praise of wealth is not couched in such magnificent poetry as Barabas's speech or Volpone's paean to gold. Like much of the speech in this play, it sounds more conversational.

[27] Lucas, *Works*, II, 218.

match.[28] He even mentions betraying a town to the Turk (III.ii.13). One might go further and note a cynicism in the fact that Marlowe's most conventional love poetry comes from the mouth of the ragged Ithamore, and many of Webster's most poetic moralizing speeches are uttered by Romelio. One might even follow Lucas and note that both Barabas and Romelio have courage in adversity and that both try to eliminate those who know too much, but these are characteristics of most of the interesting villains in the drama of the time.

In fact, this tack could lead us as far afield as Shakespeare's *Richard III*. Richard, incidentally, had burst upon the mourning Lady Anne and successfully wooed her, much as Romelio craftily talks the mourning Jolenta into pretending she is pregnant, when a hundred lines earlier she had tried to walk away from him. The mothers of both men lament that they bore such villains. And both men fool others by pretending devoutness.

Rather than yield to the temptation to hunt further parallels, we must turn back to Webster's play. It has a single thread, the scheming and downfall of Romelio, with two main movements. First, there is the attempt, by Romelio and his mother, to marry his sister Jolenta not to the debt-ridden Contarino, whom both women love, but to Ercole. The trick leads to hot words and a gentlemanly duel between the two suitors, in which both are presumably killed. Out of this grows the title event. Leonora, grieving over her surreptitious love affair, announces "Here begins/ My part i'th' play" (III.iii.380–381). Instead of plotting the typical bloodletting of revenge tragedy, however, she decides upon disinheritance, which will strike sharply at Romelio's greed. Unfortunately for her scheme, Crispiano, whom she will name in her suit, has come to Naples to investigate his son Julio's behavior, and to bear a judgeship to Ariosto. He finds himself presiding at the trial while the disgusted Ariosto tries to advise Romelio. Finally Crispiano reveals his identity, and concomitantly, the perjury of Leonora and her waiting-woman. Immediately, however, Ercole, who has recovered from his wounds, accuses Romelio of killing Contarino, who was on his deathbed when Romelio stabbed him. Another challenge and trial by combat ensues, but is broken off when Contarino's recovery is revealed. Judge Ariosto tries to sort things out at the end. He will be helped by a list of details Leonora has written down.

28 Marlowe, *Jew of Malta*, II.939 ff., in *Works*, ed. Tucker Brooke (Oxford, 1966).

Even the bare outline gives a hint of the fantastic complications of the story. Among characters with major speaking parts, only Julio, the conventional wastrel, serves little purpose, though he is an excuse for Crispiano's presence, and he attempts to echo Romelio's cynicism while providing a target for the jibes of others.

Romelio himself keeps capturing our attention. For the first time, Webster has concentrated his attention on an ambitious merchant, a man, as Contarino says, of "worthy parts . . . blasted/ By insolent vainglory" (I.i.121–122). There is, in fact, a thread of class conflict running through the play. Romelio scoffs at "gentry" as a "superstitious relic" (I.i.38–39).[29] Romelio's consistent lack of honor is in sharp contrast to the generally upright behavior of the far less interesting Ercole and Contarino. The suitors fight a duel rather than take "the way,/ Like an Italian, to cut your throat/ By practice" (II.i.265–267). Romelio does not hesitate to stab a man in his bed. Jolenta has our sympathy and a certain "hysterical truth,"[30] but we are most fascinated by the two scenes in which Romelio despicably outwits her.[31]

Greed drives him along, and his mother recognizes this. She, although not given to cynical comments, is very much like her son, while sharing with Vittoria Corombona and the Duchess of Malfi a willingness to flaunt convention. Webster seems to avoid making a moral pronouncement on either, and keeps his reader off balance by motivating Leonora's revenge plot and making it detrimental to her reputation, and by placing Romelio in a series of adverse situations. The supremely self-confident merchant hears that his ships have sunk, and our modern minds cannot share Ariosto's superstitions about their names. Romelio stabs a man and we shudder, but immediately the Surgeons blackmail him, and we discover that he has saved Contarino. He gains our sympathy when, on trial, ignorant of the charges against him, he is denounced by corrupt Contilupo. And he gains our disfavor by his treatment of Angiolella, despite her own admission of frailty, and by his scoffing at religion.

29 Ironically, it is revealed later that Contarino will be absolved of killing Ercole because of services rendered by an ancestor!

30 Rupert Brooke, *John Webster and the Elizabethan Drama* (New York, 1916), p. 115.

31 Lucas takes his earlier "Poor Jolenta . . ." (II.iii.156) as an unexpected touch of tenderness (*Works*, II, 337), but it is probably another example of Romelio's saying things for a calculated effect.

By comparison, the despicable Surgeons or the earnest Capuchin are flat, merely serving dramatic functions. Webster was obviously more interested in the three lawyers, Crispiano, Contilupo, and Ariosto. He patently dislikes the spruce, unprincipled Contilupo. Conversely, Ariosto becomes almost a spokesman for Webster. Evidently physically small, superstitious, a railer whose targets richly deserve his abuse, he is unusual: an exemplary lawyer who "will give counsel/ In honest causes gratis; never in his life/ Took fee, but he came and spake for't" (II.i.111–113). Crispiano, less sharply drawn, is equally upstanding though perhaps overly joyful at his financial success, less cynical than Ariosto, but quick of mind as he presides over the trial. He is more than a match for Winifrid, the delightfully original "old hare" whose motivations are devotion to Leonora and genuine fear when her perjury is discovered.

Although Winifrid seems English, and there are frequent references to the City and to the Dutch, Webster has set his play in the typical Englishman's notion of Renaissance Italy.[32] The common enemy is the Turk, the common condition is corruption. In a tragedy, Webster might have done much more with his images of rottenness, and of great people and mountains as deformed heaps. In tragicomedy, however, the "rotten ground" has given rise to "comical events." The devil, although mentioned frequently, inspires characters more to remediable treachery than to tragic actions.

Italians were adept at disguise, too, and in a play where appearance and reality are frequently at variance, half the main characters hide their identities. As in his tragedies, Webster thinks of disguise merely as outward covering. Romelio, in his large nose and gabardine, never changes the cadence of his speeches.[33] Crispiano's idiom is the same for merchant and for judge. A theater audience, of course, would be spared the reader's confusion at forgetting Contarino's Danish garb, and would get the full impact of Jolenta's Moorish make-up.

32 The *Contra Machiavel* of Gentillet had done much to give this warped view. Contarino sounds English rather than Italian in I.i.62–65: "I have heard/ Of divers, that in passing of the Alps,/ Have but exchang'd their virtues at dear rate/ For other vices."

33 Compare Volpone using the cant of a mountebank or Barabas in disguise. Frederick Erastus Pierce points out how little disguised people act their parts, in "The Collaboration of Webster and Dekker," *Yale Studies in English*, XXXVII (New York, 1909), p. 113.

Webster, addressing his reader, emphasized the importance of the action. While much of the visual imagery can be savored better by the reader, there is the pageantry and dueling that appealed to the groundlings, and there should be humor with Winifrid and with Sanitonella and his buckram bag. The figures arrayed at the trial and registering reactions should have great impact, too.[34] Stoll cites the trial as "a great technical advance over that in the *White Devil*; the intent of the plaintiff is but darkly hinted at, and revealed only in open court, and the identity of the judge with the co-respondent is kept back for a climax to the whole."[35]

This, of course, is one more example of the way Webster keeps his readers uncertain through so much of the play. Only with his indignation at a travesty of justice does he take a firm stand. At other times he says that appearance and reality are at variance, and he seems to accept this as a fact of life. One must often guess at a person's sincerity—there is no sure guide. Jolenta, in the last of the aphoristic passages Webster likes so much, does speak sincerely for the true beauty of the soul. But the language of the play is that of contracts, money, and accounts; and earlier Romelio has noted equally sincerely that there is little good in man, that even graves are not sacred if profit is to be made. The good people may win in *The Devil's Law-Case*, and the Capuchin may be sure Heaven had a hand in it. The bad may be punished, though "With no severity of sentence" (V.vi.64). But as outsiders, we feel that this is fortuitous, and that Webster is not making a case for a governing good principle. The apothecaries will continue to fleece the greedy gulls (II.i.198–203).[36] And women, like Leonora and Winifrid, will spend their lives "in that which least concerns life" (III.iii.410). There is cynicism not only in the mouths of the characters, but in Webster's handling of scenes, and even in the subtitle. Nowhere else in his plays is there such mocking of genuine misfortunes,[37] and such unwillingness to chart a steady course. The result is a play not so successfully dark or coherent in feeling as the tragedies, but rather a sour piece in which the

[34] For a more complete study of the play on stage, see George Fullmer Reynolds, *The Staging of Elizabethan Plays at the Red Bull Theatre, 1605–1625* (New York, 1940).

[35] Stoll, *John Webster*, p. 176.

[36] Ian Scott-Kilvert, *John Webster* (London, 1964), p. 14, points out the acceptance of the Machiavellian doctrine that men were naturally weak or wicked.

[37] Stoll, *John Webster*, p. 58.

happy moments seem almost accidents in the pattern of life. Webster seems to be commenting on more than the Englishman's Renaissance Italy.

THE TEXT

The text is the least problematic aspect of *The Devil's Law-Case.* There is only one seventeenth-century edition, the Quarto of 1623. In its corrected state, it presents relatively few difficulties—an occasional omitted letter, some misplaced stage directions, and a couple of missing words, such as the "not" that Hazlitt added at II.i.48. The original state of the Quarto was far less perfect, but corrections were made during the press run, as was then customary. Sheet G shows the most frequent compositor's lapses, ranging from a misspelled word, through misread words, to an omitted line. The Ashley Collection copy in the British Museum has a corrected G1^{v}, but includes the numerous errors of G3^{v} and G4 (III.iii.429–IV.i.64). The copy in Harvard's Houghton Library is unique in its uncorrected G4^{v}. The outer forme of K ranks next in interest, for among its four corrections is the change from "salt" to "rough" at V.i.40.

Despite the cleanness of the copy-text, an editor has one besetting difficulty: the arrangement of lines of verse. Only seldom are lines of apparent verse printed as prose. More frequently, the line divisions are quite haphazard, with one verse line running up to seven feet, and the next having only three or four feet. Part of this may be blamed on the compositor. But more frequently one feels that Webster is employing an irregular pattern that comes close to everyday speech. Rupert Brooke attributed the unevenness to Webster's bad ear for meter and characterizes the poetry well: "Each line tends to have about ten syllables and about five feet. It looks in the distance like a blank verse line."[38] Dyce, responsible for the first modern edition of the play, figuratively threw up his hands in despair as he tackled V.v.13. After suggesting that "And may I be found dead time enough" could be regularized if it read "in time," he added "But the versification of this play is in many places wretched."[39] Dyce evidently had far less difficulty in establishing the formal scene divisions that have generally been accepted in succeeding editions, including the present one.

38 Brooke, *John Webster* p. 130.
39 Dyce, *Works*, p. 143.

We cannot be sure what sort of manuscript the printer worked from. He may have had a playhouse promptbook, or he may have had the author's fair copy. John Russell Brown, although he reaches no absolute decision, leans toward an author's copy,[40] and the Quarto seems to support this. We cannot take the shift in character names, when "Waiting-Woman" becomes "Winifrid" halfway through the play, as conclusive, although it is the thing a prompter would try to avoid. He would, furthermore, be quite attentive to entrances and exits. In an otherwise carefully printed text it seems to me improbable that stage directions would have been omitted if included in the copy. If we go on to note misplaced stage directions, we find that they are about equally divided between late and early, so that there is no evidence of a prompter's anticipatory directions.

Three last bits of inconclusive evidence should be noted. Generally, theatrical copy begins speeches on new lines. In *The Devil's Law-Case*, some one-word speeches appear by themselves, others are crammed into the adjoining line, as printers frequently did to save space.[41] Brooke took the changing of "Surgeons" to "Surgeon" in speeches in III.iii, as proof of theatrical economy, but Mr. Brown rejects this.[42] After all, there are still two at the end, when sentence is passed! On the other hand, the silent presence of Baptista would be a waste of an actor, and is more likely to have survived in an author's revised copy than in a playhouse manuscript. The same could be said of the two silent Bellmen in II.iii.

Whatever the copy used by Augustine Matthews, the printer (the "A.M." of the Quarto title page), it is certain that he worked with Webster's approval, and perhaps even had his assistance. Much earlier, in his address to the Reader of *The White Devil*, Webster commented on the advantages of having a printed play for a fuller understanding. The idea that he is writing for a more select group and not the common, rather dense, audience is still present in *The Devil's Law-Case*. Webster provides a dedicatory paragraph, as well as an address to the reader, and tells us that he used restraint in not including commendatory verses urged on him by friends.

40 John Russell Brown, "The Printing of John Webster's Plays," *Studies in Bibliography*, Vols. VI (1954) and VIII (1956).

41 W. W. Greg, *Dramatic Documents from the Elizabethan Playhouse, Commentary* (London, 1931), p. 207, considers short speeches beginning on separate lines evidence of theatrical origin.

42 Brown, "Printing," VI, 137; Rupert Brooke, *John Webster* p. 259.

There are two corrections that might indicate Webster's involvement with the actual printing. At IV.i.16, the uncorrected Quarto prints "ith Margent sheet." Perhaps the typesetter's eye picked up the last word from five lines above, and the printer realized this, but excising the word "sheet" in later copies seems rather like an authoritative change. More important is the word "salt" in V.i.40, which is emended to "rough." Although this is a telling change, before we take it as proof that Webster saw the pages during printing, we must remember that there are other apparent omissions which only later editors have caught (the "not" that is essential to the sense of II.i.48; the "incision" that Dyce added in III.ii.27).

This edition is based on a complete collation of the uncorrected Quarto in the Pierpont Morgan Library, of the partially corrected copies in the Houghton Library and the British Museum, and of the more perfect copies in the Dyce Collection of the Victoria and Albert Museum and the Boston Public Library. In addition, I have compared sheets with errors to the corresponding leaves in other copies of the Quarto in the New York Public Library, the Library of Congress, the Bodleian Library at Oxford, and the Cambridge University Library.

FRANCES SHIRLEY

Wheaton College,
Norton, Mass.

THE DEVIL'S LAW-CASE

To the Right Worthy, and All-accomplish'd Gentleman, Sir Thomas Finch, Knight Baronet

Sir, let it not appear strange that I do aspire to your patronage. Things that taste of any goodness love to be shelter'd near goodness; nor do I flatter in this (which I hate) only touch at the original copy of your virtues. Some of my other works, as *The White Devil*, *The Duchess of Malfi*, *Guise*, and others, you have formerly seen; I present this humbly to kiss your hands, and to find your allowance. Nor do I much doubt it, knowing the greatest of the Caesars have cheerfully entertain'd less poems than this; and had I thought it unworthy, I had not enquired after so worthy a patronage. Your self I understand to be all courtesy. I doubt not therefore of your acceptance, but resolve that my election is happy. For which favor done me, I shall ever rest

Your Worship's humbly devoted,
JOHN WEBSTER

0.2 *Sir Thomas Finch*] Son of Sir Moyle Finch and Elizabeth Heneage Finch, first Countess of Winchilsea, he became Earl of Winchilsea in 1634.

5. *Guise*] a lost play, presumably about the assassination of the Duke of Guise in 1588 after years of French political intrigue.

To the Judicious Reader

I hold it, in these kind of poems, with that of Horace, *Sapientia prima, stultitia caruisse,* to be free from those vices which proceed from ignorance; of which, I take it, this play will ingeniously acquit itself. I do chiefly, therefore, expose it to the judicious; *locus est & pluribus umbris*— others have leave to sit down and read it, who come unbidden. But to these, should a man present them with the most excellent music, it would delight them no more than *auriculas citharae collecta sorde dolentis.* I will not further insist upon the approvement of it; for I am so far from praising myself, that I have not given way to divers of my friends, whose unbegg'd commendatory verses offered themselves to do me service in the front of this poem. A great part of the grace of this (I confess) lay in action; yet can no action ever be gracious, where the decency of the language, and ingenious structure of the scene, arrive not to make up a perfect harmony. What I have fail'd of this, you that have approved my other works (when you have read this), tax me of. For the rest, *Non ego ventosae plebis suffragia venor.*

---

1. *with that of*] in accord with that statement of.

2. *Sapientia . . . caruisse*] Horace, *Epistle* I, i, 41–42, "the beginning of wisdom is to have got rid of folly."

5. *locus . . . umbris*] Horace, *Epistle* I, v, 28, "and there is room for a number of shadows" (i.e., unbidden followers).

9. *auriculas . . . dolentis*] Horace, *Epistle* I, ii, 53, "citherns to ears that suffer from collected dirt."

19. *Non . . . venor*] Horace, *Epistle* I, xix, 37, "I am not one to hunt the votes of a fickle public."

THE ACTORS' NAMES

ROMELIO, *a merchant*
CONTARINO, *a nobleman*
CRISPIANO, *a civil lawyer*
ERCOLE, *a Knight of Malta*
ARIOSTO, *an advocate*
PROSPERO
JULIO [, *son to Crispiano*]
A CAPUCHIN
CONTILUPO [, *a lawyer*]
SANITONELLA [, *clerk to Crispiano*]
[BAPTISTA]
LEONORA [, *mother to Romelio and Jolenta*]
JOLENTA [, *sister to Romelio*]
[WINIFRID], *a waiting woman*
[ANGIOLELLA, *a nun*
TWO SURGEONS
A JUDGE
A LAWYER
TWO BELLMEN
COURT REGISTER
A MARSHAL
HERALD
TWO COURT OFFICERS
SERVANTS
ATTENDANTS]

The Scene, Naples

26.] *precedes "The Actors' Names" in Q.*

---

8. *Capuchin*] Franciscan friar of an austere order founded in 1528 and at first distinguished by a pointed hood or capuche.
19. *Bellmen*] town criers who often doubled as night watchmen.

The Devil's Law-Case or When Women go to Law, the Devil is full of Business

[I.i] *Enter* Romelio *and* Prospero.

PROSPERO.

You have shown a world of wealth; I did not think
There had been a merchant liv'd in Italy
Of half your substance.

ROMELIO.

I'll give the King of Spain
Ten thousand ducats yearly, and discharge
My yearly custom. The Hollanders scarce trade
More generally than I. My factors' wives
Wear chaperons of velvet, and my scriveners,
Merely through my employment, grow so rich
They build their palaces and belvederes
With musical water-works. Never in my life
Had I a loss at sea. They call me on th'Exchange

1–3.] *Dyce;* You . . . wealth;/ I . . . Merchant/ Liu'd . . . substance *Q*.

---

5. *ducats*] probably the gold coin worth about $2.50; the silver ducat was about one-third as valuable.

5–6. *discharge . . . custom*] Spain ruled Naples in accord with the Treaty of Cateau Cambrésis (1559) and collected taxes or customs duties.

8. *chaperons*] hoods or caps.

10. *belvederes*] summer houses with a good view.

11. *musical water-works*] ornamental contrivances, often with waterfalls or fountains, in which water powered musical instruments or artificial singing birds.

12. *Exchange*] a place where merchants assemble to transact business. In England, it was the Burse, built by Sir Thomas Gresham in 1566–1567 and subsequently called the "Royal Exchange" (*OED*).

The Fortunate Young Man, and make great suit
To venture with me. Shall I tell you, sir,
Of a strange confidence in my way of trading?
I reckon it as certain as the gain
In erecting a lottery.

PROSPERO.
I pray, sir, what do you think
Of Signior Baptisto's estate?

ROMELIO. A mere beggar:
He's worth some fifty thousand ducats.

PROSPERO.
Is not that well?

ROMELIO.
How, well? For a man to be melted to snow water
With toiling in the world from three and twenty
Till threescore, for poor fifty thousand ducats!

PROSPERO.
To your estate 'tis little, I confess;
You have the spring-tide of gold.

ROMELIO.
Faith, and for silver,
Should I not send it packing to th'East Indies,
We should have a glut on't.

Enter Servant.

SERVANT.
Here's the great Lord Contarino.

PROSPERO.
O, I know his business; he's a suitor to your sister.

ROMELIO.
Yes, sir, but to you,
As my most trusted friend, I utter it—
I will break the alliance.

PROSPERO.
You are ill-advised then;

13. Young Man] *Dyce;* Youngman *Q*.

---

27. *Faith*] a mild oath or asseveration, "by my faith."

There lives not a completer gentleman
In Italy, nor of a more ancient house.

ROMELIO.
What tell you me of gentry? 'Tis nought else
But a superstitious relic of time past;
And sift it to the true worth, it is nothing
But ancient riches; and in him, you know,
They are pitifully in the wane. He makes his color
Of visiting us so often, to sell land,
And thinks if he can gain my sister's love,
To recover the treble value.

PROSPERO.
Sure he loves her entirely, and she deserves it.

ROMELIO.
Faith, though she were
Crook'd-shoulder'd, having such a portion,
She would have noble suitors. But truth is,
I would wish my noble venturer take heed;
It may be, whiles he hopes to catch a gilt-head,
He may draw up a gudgeon.

Enter Contarino.

PROSPERO.
He's come. Sir, I will leave you. [*Exeunt* Prospero *and* Servant.]

CONTARINO.
I sent you the evidence of the piece of land
I motioned to you for the sale.

ROMELIO.
Yes.

53. S.D.] *Dyce.*

---

36. *not . . . gentleman*] no one more accomplished. Henry Peacham's *Compleat Gentleman* (1622) detailed the diverse abilities a gentleman should possess.

42–43. *color . . . land*] he makes selling land the pretense for visiting us so often.

51. *gilt-head*] perhaps the dolphin, but probably the golden wrasse or bonito, food fish.

52. *gudgeon*] a small bait fish.

54. *evidence*] title deeds.

55. *motioned*] recommended.

CONTARINO.

Has your counsel perus'd it?

ROMELIO.

Not yet, my lord. Do you intend to travel?

CONTARINO.

No.

ROMELIO.

O, then you lose
That which makes man most absolute.

CONTARINO.

Yet I have heard
Of divers, that in passing of the Alps,
Have but exchang'd their virtues at dear rate
For other vices.

ROMELIO.

O, my lord, lie not idle;
The chiefest action for a man of great spirit,
Is never to be out of action. We should think
The soul was never put into the body,
Which has so many rare and curious pieces
Of mathematical motion, to stand still.
Virtue is ever sowing of her seeds:
In the trenches for the soldier; in the wakeful study
For the scholar; in the furrows of the sea
For men of our profession: of all which
Arise and spring up honor. Come, I know
You have some noble great design in hand,
That you levy so much money.

CONTARINO.

Sir, I'll tell you:
The greatest part of it I mean to employ

62–65.] *Lucas; prose in Q.*

---

61. *absolute*] complete.

63–65. *that . . . vices*] from the English audience's point of view, traveling to Italy, where vices were traditionally acquired. Webster seems to have forgotten that the action is set in Italy.

69–71. *The soul . . . still*] Lucas quotes Sykes on the similarity to *Arcadia*, I (*Works*, I, 58).

71. *mathematical*] regular, exact.

In payment of my debts, and the remainder
Is like to bring me into greater bonds, as I aim it.

ROMELIO.
How, sir?

CONTARINO.
I intend it for the charge of my wedding.

ROMELIO.
Are you to be married, my lord?

CONTARINO.
Yes, sir; and I must now entreat your pardon
That I have concealed from you a business
Wherein you had at first been call'd to counsel,
But that I thought it a less fault in friendship
To engage myself thus far without your knowledge
Than to do it against your will. Another reason
Was, that I would not publish to the world,
Nor have it whispered scarce, what wealthy voyage
I went about, till I had got the mine
In mine own possession.

ROMELIO.
You are dark to me yet.

CONTARINO.
I'll now remove the cloud. Sir, your sister and I
Are vowed each other's, and there only wants
Her worthy mother's and your fair consents
To style it marriage. This is a way,
Not only to make a friendship, but confirm it
For our posterities. How do you look upon't?

ROMELIO.
Believe me, sir, as on the principal column
To advance our house. Why, you bring honor with you,
Which is the soul of wealth. I shall be proud
To live to see my little nephews ride
O'th' upper hand of their uncles; and the daughters

89–91. *But . . . will*] Lucas quotes Sykes on the similarity to *Arcadia*, I (*Works*, I, 86).

93–95. *what . . . possession*] calling to mind voyages to the rich mines in the New World, as well as the common idea of a voyage in conquest of one's love.

96. *You . . . me*] Your meaning is concealed from me.

Be rank'd by heralds at solemnities
Before the mother: all this deriv'd
From your nobility. Do not blame me, sir,
If I be taken with't exceedingly;
For this same honor with us citizens
Is a thing we are mainly fond of, especially
When it comes without money, which is very seldom.
But as you do perceive my present temper,
Be sure I am yours—[*aside*] fir'd with scorn and laughter
At your over-confident purpose—and no doubt,
My mother will be of your mind.

CONTARINO.

'Tis my hope, sir. *Exit* Romelio.
I do observe how this Romelio
Has very worthy parts, were they not blasted
By insolent vainglory. There rests now
The mother's approbation to the match,
Who is a woman of that state and bearing,
Though she be City-born, both in her language,
Her garments, and her table, she excels
Our ladies of the Court. She goes not gaudy,
Yet have I seen her wear one diamond
Would have bought twenty gay ones out of their clothes,
And some of them, without the greater grace,
Out of their honesties.

Enter Leonora.

She comes. I will try
How she stands affected to me, without relating
My contract with her daughter.

116. S.D.] *Dyce.*
119. S.D.] *Dyce; at l. 118 in Q.*

---

113. *mainly*] greatly.
121. *parts*] personal qualities, attributes.
125. *City-born*] to Webster's audience, one of the merchant class from the City of London proper. The Court was at Westminster, then a separate community.
126. *table*] the food provided for family or guests.
130. *without . . . grace*] without further payment, or without calling it a favor.
132. *try*] test.

LEONORA.

Sir, you are nobly welcome, and presume
You are in a place that's wholly dedicated
To your service.

CONTARINO.

I am ever bound to you for many special favors.

LEONORA.

Sir, your fame renders you most worthy of it.

CONTARINO.

It could never have got a sweeter air to fly in
Than your breath.

LEONORA.

You have been strange a long time; you are weary
Of our unseasonable time of feeding.
Indeed th'Exchange Bell makes us dine so late,
I think the ladies of the Court from us
Learn to lie so long abed.

CONTARINO.

They have a kind of Exchange among them too;
Marry, unless it be to hear of news, I take it
Theirs is, like the New Burse, thinly furnish'd
With tires and new fashions. I have a suit to you.

LEONORA.

I would not have you value it the less
If I say, 'tis granted already.

---

135. *presume*] you must presume.

140–141. *It . . . breath*] Similar lines are in Webster, *The Monumental Column*, l. 222 (Dyce), and *Arcadia*, II (Lucas).

142. *strange*] a stranger.

143–144. *our . . . late*] The merchants would not dine until the Exchange closed at noon, while others normally ate dinner earlier (Harrison, *Description of England* [1577], in Lothrop Withington, ed., *Elizabethan England*, [New York, n.d.], p. 105).

145–146. *ladies . . . abed*] Lucas points out that the citizens' wives would normally be expected to copy the Court, but that merchants' wives were lying abed till almost noon, when their husbands returned from the Exchange (Dekker, *Jests to make you merry* [1607]).

148. *Marry*] Formerly an oath, "by Mary," it had lost force by the seventeenth century.

149. *New Burse*] the New Exchange in the Strand, where women's furnishings, primarily, were sold. Intended to rival the Old Exchange (cf. l. 12, above), it was unpopular and poorly stocked in Webster's time.

150. *tires*] apparel.

CONTARINO.

You are all bounty.
'Tis to bestow your picture on me.

LEONORA.

O, sir, shadows are coveted in summer,
And with me, 'tis fall o'th' leaf.

CONTARINO.

You enjoy the best of time;
This latter spring of yours shows in my eye
More fruitful and more temperate withal,
Than that whose date is only limited
By the music of the cuckoo.

LEONORA.

Indeed, sir, I dare tell you,
My looking glass is a true one, and as yet
It does not terrify me. Must you have my picture?

CONTARINO.

So please you, lady, and I shall preserve it
As a most choice object.

LEONORA.

You will enjoin me to a strange punishment.
With what a compell'd face a woman sits
While she is drawing! I have noted divers
Either to feign smiles, or suck in the lips
To have a little mouth; ruffle the cheeks
To have the dimple seen; and so disorder
The face with affectation, at next sitting
It has not been the same; I have known others
Have lost the entire fashion of their face
In half an hour's sitting.

153–154.] *Dyce;* You . . . your/ Picture on me *Q*.

---

155. *shadows*] The pun is on the common use of the word to mean "pictures."

161. *cuckoo*] A harbinger of spring in England, the cuckoo flies south in August.

168. *compell'd*] forced, carefully constrained.

169. *is drawing*] is being drawn.

169. *divers*] various (women).

CONTARINO.

How?

LEONORA.

In hot weather,
The painting on their face has been so mellow,
They have left the poor man harder work by half
To mend the copy he wrought by; but indeed,
If ever I would have mine drawn to th' life,
I would have a painter steal it at such a time
I were devoutly kneeling at my prayers;
There is then a heavenly beauty in't: the soul
Moves in the superficies.

CONTARINO.

Excellent lady,
Now you teach beauty a preservative
More than 'gainst fading colors; and your judgment
Is perfect in all things.

LEONORA.

Indeed, sir, I am a widow,
And want the addition to make it so;
For man's experience has still been held
Woman's best eyesight. I pray, sir, tell me:
You are about to sell a piece of land
To my son, I hear.

CONTARINO.

'Tis truth.

LEONORA.

Now I could rather wish
That noblemen would ever live i'th' country,
Rather than make their visits up to th' city
About such business. O, sir, noble houses

---

179. *mellow*] soft.

186. *Moves . . . superficies*] becomes apparent, shows in the face.

192. *want the addition*] need the help of a man's added experience for perfect judgment.

193–194. *For . . . eyesight*] Lucas cites a parallel line in *Arcadia*, III (*Works*, I, 380).

198–201. *I . . . business*] Attempts were made in 1617 and 1623 to encourage landed gentry to remain in the country, rather than flock to London for fashion's sake, chiefly at the behest of their wives and daughters (Lucas).

Have no such goodly prospects any way
As into their own land; the decay of that,
Next to their begging churchland, is a ruin
Worth all men's pity. Sir, I have forty thousand crowns
Sleep in my chest, shall waken when you please,
And fly to your commands. Will you stay supper?

CONTARINO.

I cannot, worthy lady.

LEONORA.

I would not have you come hither, sir, to sell,
But to settle your estate. I hope you understand
Wherefore I make this proffer: so I leave you. *Exit* Leonora.

CONTARINO.

What a treasury have I pearch'd!
"I hope you understand wherefore I make this proffer."
She has got some intelligence, how I intend to marry
Her daughter, and ingenuously perceived
That by her picture, which I begged of her,
I meant the fair Jolenta. Here's a letter
Which gives express charge not to visit her
Till midnight: [*Reads.*]
"Fail not to come, for 'tis a business
That concerns both our honors.
Yours, in danger to be lost, Jolenta."
'Tis a strange injunction. What should be the business?
She is not chang'd, I hope. I'll thither straight;
For women's resolutions in such deeds,
Like bees, light oft on flowers, and oft on weeds. *Exit.*

211. S.D.] *Dyce; at. l. 212 in Q.* 219–220.] *Lucas; one line in Q.*
219. S.D.] *Dyce.*

---

204. *begging churchland*] Although from the Dissolution of the monasteries by Henry VIII to the reign of Charles I much of the confiscated land was sold, some of the property was given gratis (Trevelyan, I, 101), and there was greedy competition for it.

205. *crowns*] gold coins stamped with a crown, worth five shillings (about $10.00 today).

212. *pearch'd*] variant spelling of "pierced," to broach or bore into (*OED*).

215. *ingenuously*] ingeniously; "by writers of Webster's time, *ingenious* and *ingenuous* were often confounded" (Dyce).

[I.ii] *Enter* Ercole, Romelio, Jolenta.

ROMELIO.
O sister, come, the tailor must to work
To make your wedding clothes.

JOLENTA.
The tomb-maker, to take measure of my coffin.

ROMELIO.
Tomb-maker? Look you,
The King of Spain greets you.
[*Extends folded paper with seals.*]

JOLENTA.
What does this mean? Do you serve process on me?

ROMELIO.
Process? Come, you would be witty now.

JOLENTA.
Why, what's this, I pray?

ROMELIO.
Infinite grace to you: it is a letter
From his Catholic Majesty, for the commends
Of this gentleman for your husband.

JOLENTA.
In good season. I hope he will not have my
Allegiance stretch'd to the undoing of myself.

ROMELIO.
Undo yourself? He does proclaim him here—

JOLENTA.
Not for a traitor, does he?

ROMELIO.
You are not mad?
For one of the noblest gentlemen.

JOLENTA.
Yet kings many times
Know merely but men's outsides; was this commendation
Voluntary, think you?

---

6. *serve process*] serve a court summons.

12–13. *my/ Allegiance*] another reference to Spanish rule of Naples.

14–15. *proclaim . . . for a traitor*] stock phrase for announcing that a person was enemy to a state.

ROMELIO.

Voluntary? What mean you by that?

JOLENTA.

Why, I do not think but he begg'd it of the King,
And it may fortune to be out of's way:
Some better suit—that would have stood his lordship
In far more stead. Letters of commendations!
Why, 'tis reported that they are grown stale,
When places fall i'th' University.
I pray you return his pass; for to a widow
That longs to be a courtier, this paper
May do knight's service.

ERCOLE.

Mistake not, excellent mistress; these commends
Express His Majesty of Spain has given me
Both addition of honor, as you may perceive
By my habit, and a place here to command
O'er thirty galleys; this your brother shows,
As wishing that you would be partner
In my good fortune.

ROMELIO.

I pray come hither. Have I any interest in you?

JOLENTA.

You are my brother.

ROMELIO.

I would have you then use me with that respect,
You may still keep me so; and to be swayed
In this main business of life, which wants

---

23. *it may fortune*] it may chance.

25–27. *Letters . . . University*] such letters have been overused and no longer have any influence, even at the university. Lucas notes that Cambridge officials were then expressing dislike for requests for favoritism in admitting students.

28. *pass*] a testimonial giving permission to beg.

30. *knight's service*] be useful. Equivalent of "yeoman service," it also carries an overtone of the knight's obligatory feudal service, and is appropriate to the courtly ambition Jolenta is deriding.

31–32. *these commends/ Express*] these recommendations tell that.

33–35. *addition . . . galleys*] higher rank that is reflected in one's costume, as well as in an assignment to command thirty large warships.

38. *interest in*] influence over.

Greatest consideration, your marriage,
By my direction. Here's a gentleman—

JOLENTA.
Sir, I have often told you,
I am so little my own to dispose that way,
That I can never be his.

ROMELIO.
Come, too much light
Makes you moon-eyed. Are you in love with title?
I will have a herald, whose continual practice
Is all in pedigree, come a-wooing to you,
Or an antiquary in old buskins.

ERCOLE.
Sir, you have done me
The mainest wrong that e'er was offer'd
To a gentleman of my breeding.

ROMELIO.
Why, sir?

ERCOLE.
You have led me
With a vain confidence that I should marry
Your sister; have proclaim'd it to my friends;
Employ'd the greatest lawyers of our state
To settle her a jointure; and the issue
Is, that I must become ridiculous
Both to my friends and enemies. I will leave you,
Till I call to you for a strict account
Of your unmanly dealing.

ROMELIO. Stay, my lord.—
[*Aside to* Jolenta.] Do you long to have my throat cut?
—Good my lord,

66. S.D.] *Lucas.*

---

48. *light*] in this instance, the glitter of the court and the figurative glitter of titles.

49. *moon-eyed*] blind. The term, from farriery, refers to intermittent blindness supposedly caused by the moon's influence.

52. *buskins*] boots reaching to the calf or knee.

54. *mainest*] greatest.

61. *jointure*] an estate settled upon the wife to provide for her in widowhood.

Stay but a little, till I have removed
This court-mist from her eyes, till I wake her
From this dull sleep, wherein she'll dream herself
To a deformed beggar.—[*To* Jolenta.] You would marry
The great Lord Contarino—

Enter Leonora.

LEONORA. Contarino
Were you talking of? He lost last night at dice
Five thousand ducats; and when that was gone,
Set at one throw a lordship that twice trebled
The former loss.

ROMELIO.
And that flew after?

LEONORA. And most carefully
Carried the gentleman in his caroche
To a lawyer's chamber, there most legally
To put him in possession. Was this wisdom?

ROMELIO.
O yes, their credit in the way of gaming
Is the main thing they stand on; that must be paid
Though the brewer bawl for's money; and this lord
Does she prefer i'th' way of marriage
Before our choice here, noble Ercole.

LEONORA.
You'll be advis'd, I hope. Know for your sakes
I married, that I might have children;
And for your sakes, if you'll be rul'd by me,
I will never marry again. Here's a gentleman
Is noble, rich, well featur'd, but 'bove all,
He loves you entirely; his intents are aimed
For an expedition 'gainst the Turk,
Which makes the contract cannot be delayed.

70. S.D.] *Lucas.*

84. choice . . . Ercole] *Dyce;* Choyce. Here noble *Ercole Q.*

77. *caroche*] a town carriage.

84. *choice . . . Ercole*] Lucas suggests the Q punctuation may indicate that Romelio here offers Jolenta's hand to Ercole.

90. *entirely*] completely, with whole devotion.

91. *an expedition . . . Turk*] Despite defeat at Lepanto in 1571, the Turks still held Cyprus and had great sea power. In the early 1600s peace was frequently broken.

JOLENTA.

Contract? You must do this without my knowledge.
Give me some potion to make me mad,
And happily not knowing what I speak,
I may then consent to't.

ROMELIO.

Come, you are mad already,
And I shall never hear you speak good sense
Till you name him for husband.

ERCOLE.

Lady, I will do a manly office for you:
I will leave you to the freedom of your own soul.
May it move whither heaven and you please.

JOLENTA.

Now you express yourself most nobly.

ROMELIO.

Stay, sir; what do you mean to do?

LEONORA [*kneels*].

Hear me: if thou dost marry Contarino,
All the misfortune that did ever dwell
In a parent's curse, light on thee!

ERCOLE.

O, rise, lady. Certainly heaven never
Intended kneeling to this fearful purpose.

JOLENTA.

Your imprecation has undone me forever.

ERCOLE.

Give me your hand.

JOLENTA.

No, sir.

ROMELIO.

Giv't me then. [*Takes her by the hand.*]
O what rare workmanship have I seen this
To finish with your needle, what excellent music
Have these struck upon the viol!
Now I'll teach a piece of art.

JOLENTA.

Rather a damnable cunning,

105. S.D.] *Lucas.*
108–109.] *Dyce;* Oh . . . intended/ Kneeling . . . purpose *Q.*
113. S.D.] *Lucas.*

95. *happily*] haply, by chance.

To have me go about to give't away
Without consent of my soul.

ROMELIO. Kiss her, my lord.
If crying had been regarded, maidenheads
Had ne'er been lost; at least some appearance of crying,
As an April shower i'th' sunshine.

LEONORA.
She is yours.

ROMELIO.
Nay, continue your station, and deal you in
Dumb show; kiss this doggedness out of her.

LEONORA.
To be contracted in tears, is but fashionable.

ROMELIO.
Yet suppose that they were hearty—

LEONORA.
Virgins must seem unwilling.

ROMELIO.
O, what else? And you remember, we observe
The like in greater ceremonies than these contracts.
At the consecration of prelates, they use ever
Twice to say nay, and take it. [*Places her hand in Ercole's.*]

JOLENTA.
O, brother!

ROMELIO.
Keep your possession, you have the door by th' ring;
That's livery and seisin in England. But my lord,

120–123. Kiss . . . sunshine] *Lucas;* Kisse . . . regarded,/ Maidenheads . . . appearance/ Of . . . Sunshine *Q.*

130–131.] *Hazlitt;* Oh . . . the/ Like . . . Contracts *Q.*

---

125. *station*] in theatrical parlance, a playing place. For Ercole, the military man, it could also have the overtone of sticking to his post.

126. *Dumb show*] Continuing the theatrical metaphor, Romelio is urging action rather than talk.

128. *Yet*] moreover.

128. *hearty*] sincere.

132–133. *consecration . . . take it*] A bishopric was customarily refused twice pro forma, then accepted (Lucas).

135. *have . . . ring*] The possession of the latch ring or key was a token of owning a house in England.

136. *livery and seisin*] "livery of seisin" (*OED*), the delivery of possession or of a token of possession, especially in feudal England.

Kiss that tear from her lip; you'll find the rose
The sweeter for the dew.

JOLENTA.
Bitter as gall.

ROMELIO. Ay, ay, all you women,
Although you be of never so low stature,
Have gall in you most abundant; it exceeds
Your brains by two ounces. I was saying somewhat:
O, do but observe i'th' City, and you'll find
The thriftiest bargains that were ever made,
What a deal of wrangling ere they could be brought
To an upshot.

LEONORA.
Great persons do not ever come together—

ROMELIO.
With reveling faces, nor is it necessary
They should; the strangeness and unwillingness
Wears the greater state, and gives occasion that
The people may buzz and talk of't, though the bells
Be tongue-tied at the wedding.

LEONORA.
And truly I have heard say,
To be a little strange to one another
Will keep your longing fresh.

ROMELIO.
Ay, and make you beget
More children when y'are married: some doctors
Are of that opinion. You see, my lord, we are merry
At the contract; your sport is to come hereafter.

ERCOLE.
I will leave you, excellent lady, and withal
Leave a heart with you so entirely yours,
That I protest, had I the least of hope
To enjoy you, though I were to wait the time
That scholars do in taking their degree
In the noble arts, 'twere nothing; howsoe'er,
He parts from you that will depart from life

146. *upshot*] conclusion.
150. *Wears . . . state*] presents the more impressive appearance.
163–165. *time . . . arts*] seven years.

To do you any service; and so humbly
I take my leave.

JOLENTA.
Sir, I will pray for you. *Exit* Ercole.

ROMELIO.
Why, that's well; 'twill make your prayer complete,
To pray for your husband.

JOLENTA.
Husband?

LEONORA.
This is the happiest hour that I ever arrived at. [*Exit* Leonora.]

ROMELIO.
Husband, ay, husband. Come, you peevish thing,
Smile me a thank for the pains I have ta'en.

JOLENTA.
I hate myself for being thus enforc'd:
You may soon judge then what I think of you,
Which are the cause of it.

Enter Waiting Woman [Winifrid].

ROMELIO.
You, lady of the laundry, come hither.

WINIFRID.
Sir?

ROMELIO.
Look, as you love your life, you have an eye
Upon your mistress; I do henceforth bar her
All visitants. I do hear there are bawds abroad
That bring cutworks and mantoons, and convey letters
To such young gentlewomen; and there are others

169. S.D.] *Dyce; at l. 168 in Q.*
180. S.P. WINIFRID] *Dyce; Wayt. Q (so to end of scene in Q).*
184. mantoons] *Q(corr.)*; Man-oons *Q(uncorr.)*.

---

174. *peevish*] obstinate.

181–192.] The first five lines especially, and the tone of the whole speech, have a precedent in Jonson's *The Devil is an Ass*, ed. Herford and Simpson, II.i.155–167.

184. *cutworks*] embroidery with the edges cut around the pattern.

184. *mantoons*] cloaks, long robes, or upper mantles (Florio).

That deal in corn-cutting and fortune-telling.
Let none of these come at her on your life;
Nor Dewes-ace, the wafer-woman, that prigs abroad
With muskmelons and malakatoones; nor
The Scotchwoman with the cittern, do you mark;
Nor a dancer by any means, though he ride on's footcloth;
Nor a hackney coachman, if he can speak French.

WINIFRID.
Why, sir?

ROMELIO.
By no means; no more words!
Nor the woman with maribone puddings. I have heard
Strange juggling tricks have been convey'd to a woman
In a pudding. You are apprehensive?

WINIFRID.
O, good sir, I have travel'd.

ROMELIO.
When you had a bastard, you travel'd indeed.
But, my precious chaperoness,
I trust thee the better for that; for I have heard
There is no warier keeper of a park,
To prevent stalkers, or your night-walkers,
Than such a man as in his youth has been
A most notorious deer-stealer.

189–190.] *Dyce;* With . . . Malakatoones;/ Nor . . . marke *Q*.

200. chaperoness] *Dyce;* Chaperoones *Q*.

---

188. *Dewes-ace, the wafer-woman*] Jonson speaks of letters conveyed by "old crones with wafers" (thin cakes), and Lucas notes a similar passage in *The Maid in the Mill*, I.ii. The proper name puns on the deuce-ace throw of dice, which is bad luck (*OED*).

188. *prigs abroad*] haggles over prices as she moves about town.

189. *malakatoones*] A melocoton was a peach grafted onto a quince (*OED*) or a kind of late peach (Gerard).

190. *cittern*] musical instrument similar to a guitar.

191. *footcloth*] ornamented cloth over a horse's back and hanging down its sides.

195. *maribone puddings*] puddings made with marrow.

196. *juggling*] cheating or deceiving.

197. *apprehensive*] perceptive.

198–199. *travel'd*] "Travel" and "travail" were originally the same word, with interchangeable spellings in the seventeenth century (*OED*).

203. *night-walker*] Criminal intentions are usually implied (*OED*).

WINIFRID.

Very well, sir,
You may use me at your pleasure.

ROMELIO.

By no means, Winifrid; that were the way
To make thee travel again. Come, be not angry,
I do but jest—thou knowest, wit and a woman
Are two very frail things—and so I leave you. *Exit.*

WINIFRID.

I could weep with you; but 'tis no matter,
I can do that at any time. I have now
A greater mind to rail a little: plague of these
Unsanctified matches! They make us loath
The most natural desire our grandame Eve ever left us.
Force one to marry against their will! —Why, 'tis
A more ungodly work than enclosing the commons.

JOLENTA.

Prithee, peace!
This is indeed an argument so common,
I cannot think of matter new enough
To express it bad enough.

Enter Contarino.

WINIFRID.

Here's one, I hope, will put you out of't.

CONTARINO.

How now, sweet mistress?
You have made sorrow look lovely of late:
You have wept.

WINIFRID.

She has done nothing else these three days. Had you stood behind the arras, to have heard her shed so much salt water

222.1.] *this edn.; after l. 223 in Q.*
227. three] *Q(corr.)*; thee *Q(uncorr.)*.

218. *enclosing the commons*] Winifrid is a bit old-fashioned: feeling against enclosure was stronger under the Tudors than under the Stuarts (Trevelyan, II, 141).

228. *arras*] large tapestry hangings a foot or two from the walls.

as I have done, you would have thought she had been turn'd fountain.

CONTARINO.

I would fain know the cause can be worthy this
Thy sorrow.

JOLENTA.

Reach me the caskanet. I am studying, sir,
To take an inventory of all that's mine.

CONTARINO.

What to do with it, lady?

JOLENTA.

To make you a deed of gift.

CONTARINO.

That's done already; you are all mine.

WINIFRID.

Yes, but the devil would fain put in for's share,
In likeness of a separation.

JOLENTA.

O, sir, I am bewitch'd.

CONTARINO.

Hah?

JOLENTA.

Most certain: I am forespoken
To be married to another; can you ever think
That I shall ever thrive in't? Am I not then bewitch'd?
All comfort I can teach myself is this:
There is a time left for me to die nobly,
When I cannot live so.

CONTARINO.

Give me, in a word, to whom, or by whose means
Are you thus torn from me?

JOLENTA.

By Lord Ercole, my mother, and my brother.

250. my brother] *Dyce;* by Brother *Q.*

---

233. *caskanet*] here, probably a jewel box. The word, a melding of carcanet (heavy necklace) and casket, can mean either (*OED*).

242. *forespoken*] spoken for in advance. The word play grows from the similarity to "forspoken," meaning "bewitched" (*OED*).

246–247. *There . . . so*] Lucas cites a parallel speech in *Arcadia,* III (*Works,* I, 508).

CONTARINO.
I'll make his bravery fitter for a grave
Than for a wedding.

JOLENTA.
So you will beget
A far more dangerous and strange disease
Out of the cure. You must love him again
For my sake: for the noble Ercole
Had such a true compassion for my sorrow—
Hark in your ear, I'll show you his right worthy
Demeanor to me.

WINIFRID [*aside*].
O, you pretty ones!
I have seen this lord many a time and oft
Set her in's lap, and talk to her of love
So feelingly, I do protest it has made me
Run out of myself to think on't.
O sweet-breath'd monkey! How they grow together!
Well, 'tis my opinion,
He was no woman's friend that did invent
A punishment for kissing.

CONTARINO.
If he bear himself so nobly,
The manliest office I can do for him
Is to afford him my pity, since he's like
To fail of so dear a purchase. For your mother,
Your goodness quits her ill. For your brother,
He that vows friendship to a man, and proves
A traitor, deserves rather to be hang'd

260. S.D.] *Lucas.*
264–266.] *Dyce;* Run . . . breath'd/ Monkey . . . opinion *Q.*

---

251. *bravery*] fine clothes.

265. *sweet-breath'd monkey*] Monkeys traditionally had aromatic breaths (Lucas). "Monkey" was also "a term of playful contempt" for a younger person (*OED*), and appropriate coming from Winifrid.

267–268. *He . . . kissing*] perhaps an allusion to Cato the Elder, who punished Manilius for kissing his own wife in the daytime and in the presence of their daughter (Lucas).

272. *purchase*] acquisition with some difficulty.

273. *quits her ill*] requites her evil.

Than he that counterfeits money; yet for your sake
I must sign his pardon too. Why do you tremble?
Be safe, you are now free from him.

JOLENTA.
O, but sir,
The intermission from a fit of an ague
Is grievous, for indeed it doth prepare us
To entertain torment next morning.

CONTARINO.
Why, he's gone to sea.

JOLENTA.
But he may return too soon.

CONTARINO.
To avoid which, we will instantly be married.

WINIFRID.
To avoid which, get you instantly to bed together,
Do, and I think no civil lawyer for his fee
Can give you better counsel.

JOLENTA.
Fie upon thee; prithee, leave us. [*Exit* Winifrid.]

CONTARINO.
Be of comfort, sweet mistress.

JOLENTA.
On one condition: we may have no quarrel about this.

CONTARINO.
Upon my life, none.

JOLENTA.
None, upon your honor?

CONTARINO.
With whom? With Ercole?
You have delivered him guiltless.
With your brother? He's part of yourself.
With your complemental mother?
I use not fight with women.
Tomorrow we'll be married.
Let those that would oppose this union

---

287. *civil lawyer*] perhaps a pun, since "civil" also meant "obliging" (Lucas).

297. *complemental*] accomplished.

298. *use not*] am not accustomed to.

Grow ne'er so subtle, and entangle themselves
In their own work like spiders; while we two
Haste to our noble wishes, and presume
The hindrance of it will breed more delight,
As black copartiments show gold more bright. *Exeunt.*

Finis Actus Primi.

[II.i] *Enter* Crispiano [*disguised*], Sanitonella.

CRISPIANO.

Am I well habited?

SANITONELLA.

Exceeding well: any man would take you for a merchant; but pray, sir, resolve me, what should be the reason that you, being one of the most eminent civil lawyers in Spain, and but newly arrived from the East Indies, should take this habit of a merchant upon you?

CRISPIANO.

Why, my son lives here in Naples, and in's riot
Doth far exceed the exhibition I allowed him.

SANITONELLA.

So then, and in this disguise you mean to trace him?

CRISPIANO.

Partly for that, but there is other business
Of greater consequence.

SANITONELLA.

Faith, for his expense, 'tis nothing to your estate: what to Don Crispiano, the famous Corregidor of Seville, who by his mere practice of the law, in less time than half a jubilee, hath gotten thirty thousand ducats a year?

305. show] *Dyce;* shewes *Q.*

---

305. *copartiments*] compartments; here, dark areas that were used for contrast in decorating.

[II.i]

1. *habited*] dressed.

7. *riot*] dissipation, extravagant living.

8. *exhibition*] allowance.

13. *Corregidor*] chief magistrate. Sykes says it can mean a mere advocate (Lucas).

13. *of*] perhaps "from," since Crispiano's travels in the Indies seem incompatible with a municipal post.

14. *jubilee*] fifty years.

CRISPIANO.

Well, I will give him line;
Let him run on in's course of spending.

SANITONELLA.

Freely?

CRISPIANO.

Freely.
For I protest, if that I could conceive
My son would take more pleasure or content,
By any course of riot, in the expense
Than I took joy, nay, soul's felicity,
In the getting of it, should all the wealth I have
Waste to as small an atomy as flies
I'th' sun, I do protest on that condition,
It should not move me.

SANITONELLA.

How's this? Cannot he take more pleasure in spending it riotously than you have done by scraping it together? O, ten thousand times more, and I make no question, five hundred young gallants will be of my opinion.
Why, all the time of your collectionship
Has been a perpetual calendar: begin first
With your melancholy study of the law
Before you came to finger the ruddocks; after that
The tiring importunity of clients,
To rise so early, and sit up so late;
You made yourself half ready in a dream,
And never prayed but in your sleep. Can I think
That you have half your lungs left with crying out
For judgments and days of trial? Remember, sir,
How often have I borne you on my shoulder,

28. pleasure] *Dyce;* peasure *Q*.
35. came] *Dyce;* come *Q*.

---

25. *atomy*] speck.
30. *make no question*] have no doubt.
32. *collectionship*] money-getting.
33. *perpetual calendar*] daily affair.
35. *ruddocks*] slang for gold or money (*OED*), coming from the notion that gold was red (Hazlitt).
38. *made . . . ready*] half dressed yourself.

Among a shoal or swarm of reeking night caps,
When that your worship has bepiss'd yourself,
Either with vehemency of argument,
Or being out from the matter. I am merry.

CRISPIANO.
Be so.

SANITONELLA.
You could not eat like a gentleman, at leisure,
But swallow'd it like flap-dragons, as if you had lived
With chewing the cud after.

CRISPIANO.
No pleasure in the world was comparable to't.

SANITONELLA.
Possible?

CRISPIANO.
He shall never taste the like, unless he study law.

SANITONELLA.
What, not in wenching, sir?
'Tis a court game, believe it,
As familiar as gleek, or any other.

CRISPIANO.
Wenching? O fie, the disease follows it.
Beside, can the fing'ring taffeties, or lawns,
Or a painted hand, or a breast, be like the pleasure
In taking clients' fees, and piling them
In several goodly rows before my desk?
And according to the bigness of each heap,
Which I took by a leer—for lawyers do not tell them—
I vail'd my cap, and withal gave great hope
The cause should go on their sides.

48. not] *Hazlitt; omitted in Q.*
49. swallow'd] *Dyce;* swallow *Q.*

---

43. *night caps*] lawyers (Lucas); see IV.i.68 and note.
46. *out . . . matter*] on the wrong track in a legal argument.
49. *swallow'd . . . flap-dragons*] at a gulp; from the game of "flap-dragon" —quickly drinking burning bits, often raisins, from brandy.
56. *gleek*] a three-handed card game.
58. *taffeties, or lawns*] shiny silk or fine linen cloths.
63. *took by a leer*] calculated at a glance.
63. *tell*] count.
64. *vail'd*] doffed.

SANITONELLA.
What think you then
Of a good cry of hounds? It has been known
Dogs have hunted lordships to a fault.

CRISPIANO.
Cry of curs!
The noise of clients at my chamber door
Was sweeter music far, in my conceit,
Than all the hunting in Europe.

SANITONELLA.
Pray, stay, sir;
Say he should spend it in good house-keeping.

CRISPIANO.
Ay, marry, sir, to have him keep a good house,
And not sell't away—I'd find no fault with that.
But his kitchen I'd have no bigger than a saw-pit;
For the smallness of a kitchen, without question,
Makes many noblemen, in France and Spain,
Build the rest of the house the bigger.

SANITONELLA.
Yes, mock-beggars.

CRISPIANO.
Some sevenscore chimneys,
But half of them have no tunnels.

SANITONELLA.
A pox upon them, cuckshaws that beget
Such monsters without fundaments!

CRISPIANO.
Come, come, leave citing other vanities;
For neither wine, nor lust, nor riotous feasts,

---

67. *cry*] pack.

68. *hunted . . . fault*] driven to a loss. In hunting, a *fault* is a check caused by losing the scent; here, financial ruin.

71. *conceit*] opinion.

77. *saw-pit*] the narrow pit where one man stood to pull the lower handle of a two-man saw.

81. *mock-beggars*] "fine, but inhospitable houses" (Lucas).

83. *tunnels*] flues.

84. *cuckshaws*] kickshaws, frivolous people; from the French *quelque chose* (*OED*).

85. *fundaments*] foundations.

Rich clothes, nor all the pleasure that the devil
Has ever practic'd with to raise a man
To a devil's likeness, e'er brought man that pleasure
I took in getting my wealth: so I conclude.
If he can out-vie me, let it fly to th' devil.
Yon's my son; what company keeps he?

Enter Romelio, Julio, Ariosto, *Baptista.*

SANITONELLA.
The gentleman he talks with
Is Romelio, the merchant.

CRISPIANO.
I never saw him till now;
'A has a brave sprightly look. I knew his father,
And sojourn'd in his house two years together
Before this young man's birth. I have news to tell him
Of certain losses happened him at sea,
That will not please him.

SANITONELLA.
What's that dapper fellow
In the long stocking? I do think 'twas he
Came to your lodging this morning.

CRISPIANO.
'Tis the same;
There he stands, but a little piece of flesh.
But he is the very miracle of a lawyer,
One that persuades men to peace, and compounds quarrels
Among his neighbors, without going to law.

SANITONELLA.
And is he a lawyer?

CRISPIANO.
Yes, and will give counsel
In honest causes gratis; never in his life
Took fee, but he came and spake for't; is a man
Of extreme practice; and yet all his longing
Is to become a judge.

102. What's] *Dyce;* What *Q.*

---

97. *'A*] he (virtually obsolete form).
97. *brave*] fine, handsome.
108. *compounds*] settles.
114. *Of extreme practice*] with a large practice.

SANITONELLA.

Indeed that's a rare longing with men of his profession. I think he'll prove the miracle of a lawyer indeed.

ROMELIO.

Here's the man brought word your father died i'th'Indies.

JULIO.

He died in perfect memory I hope,
And made me his heir.

CRISPIANO.

Yes, sir.

JULIO.

He's gone the right way, then, without question.
Friend, in time of mourning, we must not use any action
That is but accessory to the making men merry;
I do therefore give you nothing for your good tidings.

CRISPIANO.

Nor do I look for it, sir.

JULIO.

Honest fellow, give me thy hand; I do not think but thou hast carried New Year's gifts to th' Court in thy days, and learn'dst there to be so free of thy pains-taking.

ROMELIO.

Here's an old gentleman says he was chamberfellow to your father when they studied the law together at Barcelona.

JULIO.

Do you know him?

ROMELIO.

Not I: he's newly come to Naples.

JULIO.

And what's his business?

ROMELIO.

'A says he's come to read you good counsel.

CRISPIANO.

To him, rate him soundly. *This is spoke aside.*

JULIO.

And what's your counsel?

ARIOSTO.

Why, I would have you leave your whoring.

---

129. *chamberfellow*] roommate, with overtones of sharing rooms or chambers at an English inn of court.

135. *rate*] scold, berate.

JULIO.

He comes hotly upon me at first. Whoring?

ARIOSTO.

O young quat, incontinence is plagued
In all the creatures of the world!

JULIO.

When did you ever hear that a cock sparrow
Had the French pox?

ARIOSTO.

When did you ever know any of them fat, but in the nest? Ask all your cantharide-mongers that question; remember yourself, sir.

JULIO.

A very fine naturalist! A physician, I take you, by your round slop; for 'tis just of the bigness, and no more, of the case for a urinal. 'Tis concluded, you are a physician.

[Ariosto *takes off his hat.*]

What do you mean, sir? You'll take cold.

ARIOSTO.

'Tis concluded, you are a fool, a precious one. You are a mere stick of sugar candy: a man may look quite through you.

[Julio *takes off his hat.*]

JULIO.

You are a very bold gamester.

ARIOSTO.

I can play at chess, and know how to handle a rook.

JULIO.

Pray preserve your velvet from the dust.

148.1.] *Lucas.*
152.1.] *Lucas.*

---

139. *quat*] a boil; "applied contemptuously to a young person" (*OED*).

141–142. *cock sparrow . . . pox*] In "Overbury's" *Characters*, "Newes from the verie Countrie," sparrows, who never get the pox despite their proverbial salaciousness, are cited in defense of intemperate behavior (Lucas).

144. *cantharide-mongers*] sellers of cantharides—dried beetles which have diuretic, aphrodisiac, or even poisonous effects when swallowed, and raise blisters when applied externally.

147. *slop*] probably baggy breeches, although it could be a smock.

150. *precious*] out-and-out.

154. *rook*] in chess, the castle; also, a simpleton.

ARIOSTO.

Keep your hat upon the block, sir,
'Twill continue fashion the longer.

JULIO.

I was never so abused with the hat in the hand
In my life.

ARIOSTO.

I will put on—why, look you, [*Both don hats.*]
Those lands that were the client's are now become
The lawyer's; and those tenements that were
The country gentleman's, are now grown
To be his tailor's.

JULIO.

Tailor's?

ARIOSTO.

Yes, tailors in France. They grow to great
Abominable purchase, and become great officers.
How many ducats think you he has spent
Within a twelvemonth, besides his father's allowance?

JULIO.

Besides my father's allowance?
Why, gentlemen, do you think an auditor begat me?
Would you have me make even at year's end?

ROMELIO.

A hundred ducats a month in breaking Venice glasses!

ARIOSTO.

He learnt that of an English drunkard,
And a knight too, as I take it.
This comes of your numerous wardrobe.

171. gentlemen] *Hazlitt;* Gentleman *Q.*

---

156. *upon the block*] Ariosto implies that Julio's head is like the wooden blocks used to shape hats.

160. *put on*] (1) continue; (2) don a hat.

161–164. *Those . . . his tailor's*] Sykes notes a parallel passage in Jonson, *The Devil is an Ass*, II.i (Lucas).

162. *tenements*] houses.

167. *purchase*] property, with an overtone of "booty."

173. *breaking Venice glasses*] It was customary to smash one's glass after a toast; Venice was famous for her glassware.

ROMELIO.

Ay, and wearing cutwork, a pound a purl.

ARIOSTO.

Your dainty embroidered stockings,
With overblown roses to hide your gouty ankles.

ROMELIO.

And wearing more taffety for a garter, than would serve the galley dung-boat for streamers.

ARIOSTO.

Your switching up at the horse race with the *illustrissimi.*

ROMELIO.

And studying a puzzling arithmetic at the cockpit.

ARIOSTO.

Shaking your elbow at the taule-board.

ROMELIO.

And resorting to your whore in hir'd velvet,
With a spangled copper fringe at her netherlands.

ARIOSTO.

Whereas if you had stayed at Padua, and fed upon
Cow trotters and fresh beef to supper—

JULIO.

How I am baited!

ARIOSTO.

Nay, be not you so forward with him neither, for 'tis thought you'll prove a main part of his undoing.

JULIO [*aside*].

I think this fellow is a witch.

ROMELIO.

Who, I, sir?

192. S.D.] *Lucas.*

177. *pound*] English currency unit then roughly equal in purchasing power to $40 today.

177. *purl*] a loop of embroidery, often of silver or gold wire thread.

179. *overblown roses*] very full rosettes on shoe fronts.

182. *switching up*] riding up with a flourish, using a whip.

182. *illustrissimi*] Italian nobility.

183. *puzzling arithmetic*] elaborate betting odds.

184. *Shaking . . . taule-board*] shaking out dice at the table- or backgammon-board.

186. *spangled copper fringe*] worthless trim imitating gold.

187. *Padua*] the university in that city.

ARIOSTO.

You have certain rich city chuffs, that when they have no acres of their own, they will go and plow up fools, and turn them into excellent meadow; besides some enclosures for the first cherries in the spring, and apricocks to pleasure a friend at Court with. You have 'pothecaries deal in selling commodities to young gallants, will put four or five coxcombs into a sieve, and so drum with them upon their counter, they'll searce them through like Guinea pepper: they cannot endure to find a man like a pair of terriers; they would undo him in a trice.

ROMELIO.

Maybe there are such.

ARIOSTO.

O terrible exactors, fellows with six hands and three heads!

JULIO.

Ay, those are hellhounds.

ARIOSTO.

Take heed of them, they'll rent thee like tenterhooks. Hark in your ear, there is intelligence upon you: the report goes, there has been gold convey'd beyond the sea in hollow anchors.

197–198. and . . . with] *Dyce; one line of verse in Q.*

205.] *Dyce;* O . . . hands,/ And . . . heads *Q.*

194. *chuffs*] misers.

198–199. *selling commodities*] lending overvalued commodities at interest to hopeful young men who tried to sell at a profit and lost money (Lucas).

199–200. *coxcombs*] fools. The name derives from the shape of the court fool's cap, which often resembled a cock's comb.

201. *searce*] sift.

201. *Guinea pepper*] a ground pepper-like spice from West Africa.

202. *cannot . . . terriers*] lack the patience to pursue painstakingly as terriers dig after quarry.

203. *trice*] moment.

205–206. *three heads . . . hellhounds*] Cerberus, watchdog of the Classical underworld, had three heads.

207. *tenterhooks*] hooked spikes that hold stretched cloth on frames or tenters during manufacture.

208. *intelligence upon*] information about.

209. *gold . . . anchors*] Great excitement was aroused in 1618–1619, when foreign merchants were tried for smuggling gold out of England (Lucas).

Farewell; you shall know me better. I will do thee more good than thou art aware of. *Exit* Ariosto.

JULIO.

He's a mad fellow.

SANITONELLA.

He would have made an excellent barber,
He does so curry it with his tongue. *Exit.*

CRISPIANO.

Sir, I was directed to you.

ROMELIO.

From whence?

CRISPIANO.

From the East Indies.

ROMELIO.

You are very welcome.

CRISPIANO.

Please you walk apart,
I shall acquaint you with particulars
Touching your trading i'th' East Indies.

ROMELIO.

Willingly; pray walk sir. *Exeunt* Crispiano, Romelio.

Enter Ercole.

ERCOLE.

O my right worthy friends, you have stayed me long.
One health, and then aboard; for all the galleys
Are come about.

Enter Contarino.

CONTARINO.

Signior Ercole,
The wind has stood my friend, sir, to prevent
Your putting to sea.

ERCOLE.

Pray why, sir?

211. S.D.] *Lucas; at l. 212 in Q.*
223–225.] *Dyce; prose in Q.*

213–214. *barber . . . curry*] The word play is on *curry*, to comb, since Ariosto's speeches were more a "raking over" than a currying of favor.

CONTARINO.
Only love, sir;
That I might take my leave, sir, and withal
Entreat from you a private recommends
To a friend in Malta. 'Twould be delivered
To your bosom, for I had no time to write.

ERCOLE.
Pray leave us, gentlemen. *Exeunt* [Julio *and Baptista*].
Wilt please you sit? *They sit down.*

CONTARINO.
Sir, my love to you has proclaim'd you one,
Whose word was still led by a noble thought,
And that thought followed by as fair a deed.
Deceive not that opinion—we were students
At Padua together, and have long
To th' world's eye shown like friends—
Was it hearty on your part to me?

ERCOLE.
Unfeigned.

CONTARINO.
You are false
To the good thought I held of you, and now
Join the worst part of man to you, your malice,
To uphold that falsehood; sacred innocence
Is fled your bosom. Signior, I must tell you,
To draw the picture of unkindness truly
Is to express two that have dearly loved,
And fall'n at variance. 'Tis a wonder to me,
Knowing my interest in the fair Jolenta,
That you should love her.

ERCOLE.
Compare her beauty and my youth together,
And you will find the fair effects of love
No miracle at all.

CONTARINO. Yes, it will prove
Prodigious to you. I must stay your voyage.

235. S.D.] *Dyce; Exeunt Q.*
257–258. Yes . . . voyage] *Dyce;* Yes . . . you./ I . . . Voyage *Q.*

243. *hearty*] sincere. Cf. I.ii.128.
258. *Prodigious*] ominous.

ERCOLE.

Your warrant must be mighty.

CONTARINO.

T'as a seal from heaven
To do it, since you would ravish from me
What's there entitled mine. And yet I vow,
By the essential front of spotless virtue,
I have compassion of both our youths;
To approve which, I have not ta'en the way,
Like an Italian, to cut your throat
By practice, that had given you now for dead,
And never frown'd upon you.

ERCOLE.

You deal fair, sir.

CONTARINO.

Quit me of one doubt, pray, sir.

ERCOLE.

Move it.

CONTARINO.

'Tis this:
Whether her brother were a main instrument
In her design for marriage.

ERCOLE.

If I tell truth, you will not credit me.

CONTARINO.

Why?

ERCOLE.

I will tell you truth,
Yet show some reason you have not to believe me.
Her brother had no hand in't: is't not hard
For you to credit this? For you may think
I count it baseness to engage another
Into my quarrel; and for that take leave

---

263. *essential front*] the face, which expresses the most intrinsic qualities.

266–267. *Like . . . practice*] Italians were notorious for their trickery and dishonorable devices. Compare Contarino's contradictory statement at ll. 316–318.

To dissemble the truth. Sir, if you will fight
With any but myself, fight with her mother;
She was the motive.

CONTARINO.
I have no enemy in the world, then, but yourself;
You must fight with me.

ERCOLE.
I will, sir.

CONTARINO.
And instantly.

ERCOLE.
I will haste before you, point whither.

CONTARINO.
Why, you speak nobly; and for this fair dealing,
Were the rich jewel which we vary for
A thing to be divided, by my life,
I would be well content to give you half;
But since 'tis vain to think we can be friends,
'Tis needful one of us be ta'en away
From being the other's enemy.

ERCOLE.
Yet, methinks, this looks not like a quarrel.

CONTARINO.
Not a quarrel?

ERCOLE.
You have not appareled your fury well:
It goes too plain, like a scholar.

CONTARINO.
It is an ornament
Makes it more terrible, and you shall find it
A weighty injury, and attended on
By discreet valor. Because I do not strike you,
Or give you the lie—such foul preparatives
Would show like the stale injury of wine—

302–303.] *Dyce;* It . . . terrible,/ And . . . it *Q*.

285. *motive*] instigator.
292. *vary for*] are at variance over.
306. *preparatives*] preliminaries.

I reserve my rage to sit on my sword's point,
Which a great quantity of your best blood
Cannot satisfy.

ERCOLE.
You promise well to yourself.
Shall's have no seconds?

CONTARINO.
None, for fear of prevention.

ERCOLE.
The length of our weapons?

CONTARINO.
We'll fit them by the way.
So whether our time calls us to live or die,
Let us do both like noble gentlemen
And true Italians.

ERCOLE.
For that let me embrace you. [*Embraces* Contarino.]

CONTARINO.
Methinks, being an Italian, I trust you
To come somewhat too near me;
But your jealousy gave that embrace to try
If I were armed, did it not?

ERCOLE.
No, believe me,
I take your heart to be sufficient proof,
Without a privy coat; and, for my part,
A taffety is all the shirt of mail
I am armed with.

CONTARINO.
You deal equally! *Exeunt.*

Enter Julio *and* Servant.

---

313. *prevention*] Official English feeling ran against dueling, and the ritual of involving others as attendants might attract attention and forestall the match.

322. *jealousy*] suspicion.

325–326. *sufficient . . . coat*] sufficiently strong and courageous without any secret armor.

327. *taffety . . . mail*] a silk shirt is all the armor.

329. *equally*] fairly.

JULIO.

Where are these gallants, the brave Ercole
And noble Contarino?

SERVANT.

They are newly gone, sir,
And bade me tell you that they will return
Within this half hour.

Enter Romelio.

JULIO.

Met you the Lord Ercole?

ROMELIO.

No, but I met the devil in villainous tidings.

JULIO.

Why, what's the matter?

ROMELIO.

O, I am pour'd out like water! The greatest
Rivers i'th' world are lost in the sea,
And so am I! Pray leave me.
Where's Lord Ercole?

JULIO.

You were scarce gone hence, but in came Contarino.

ROMELIO.

Contarino?

JULIO.

And entreated some private conference with Ercole,
And on the sudden they have given's the slip.

ROMELIO.

One mischief never comes alone:
They are gone to fight.

JULIO.

To fight?

ROMELIO.

And you be gentlemen,
Do not talk, but make haste after them.

JULIO.

Let's take several ways then,
And if't be possible for women's sakes—
For they are proper men—use our endeavors,
That the prick do not spoil them. *Exeunt.*

[II.ii] *Enter* Ercole, Contarino.

CONTARINO.
You'll not forgo your interest in my mistress?
ERCOLE.
My sword shall answer that; come, are you ready?
CONTARINO.
Before you fight, sir, think upon your cause;
It is a wondrous foul one, and I wish
That all your exercise, these four days past,
Had been employ'd in a most fervent prayer,
And the foul sin for which you are to fight
Chiefly remember'd in't.
ERCOLE. I'd as soon take
Your counsel in divinity at this present,
As I would take a kind direction from you
For the managing my weapon; and indeed,
Both would show much alike.
Come, are you ready?
CONTARINO. Bethink yourself,
How fair the object is that we contend for.
ERCOLE.
O, I cannot forget it. *They fight.*
CONTARINO [*wounding* Ercole]. You are hurt.
ERCOLE.
Did you come hither only to tell me so,
Or to do it? I mean well, but 'twill not thrive.
CONTARINO.
Your cause, your cause, sir:
Will you yet be a man of conscience, and make
Restitution for your rage upon your deathbed?
ERCOLE.
Never, till the grave gather one of us. *Fight.*
CONTARINO [*wounding* Ercole].
That was fair, and home, I think.
ERCOLE.
You prate as if you were in a fence-school.

---

9. *present*] time.
17. *I . . . thrive*] I try to hurt you, but do not succeed.
22. *fair, and home*] a fair thrust that hit its mark.

CONTARINO.
Spare your youth, have compassion on yourself.

ERCOLE.
When I am all in pieces! I am now unfit
For any lady's bed; take the rest with you.

Contarino *wounded, falls upon* Ercole.

CONTARINO.
I am lost in too much daring. Yield your sword.

ERCOLE.
To the pangs of death I shall, but not to thee.

CONTARINO.
You are now at my repairing or confusion;
Beg your life.

ERCOLE.
O most foolishly demanded!
To bid me beg that which thou canst not give. [Ercole *faints*.]

Enter Romelio, Prospero, *Baptista*, Ariosto, Julio.

PROSPERO.
See, both of them are lost; we come too late.

ROMELIO.
Take up the body and convey it
To Saint Sebastian's monastery.

CONTARINO.
I will not part with his sword; I have won't.

JULIO.
You shall not.—
Take him up gently: so, and bow his body,
For fear of bleeding inward.
Well, these are perfect lovers.

PROSPERO.
Why, I pray?

JULIO.
It has been ever my opinion,
That there are none love perfectly indeed,
But those that hang or drown themselves for love.

32. S.D.] *Hazlitt.*

---

29. *at . . . confusion*] "at my mercy, to mend or undo you" (Hazlitt).
35. *Saint Sebastian's monastery*] appropriate, since the saint was a third-century Christian left for dead and later discovered to be alive.

Now these have chose a death next to beheading:
They have cut one another's throats,
Brave valiant lads.

PROSPERO.
Come, you do ill, to set the name of valor
Upon a violent and mad despair.
Hence may all learn, that count such actions well,
The roots of fury shoot themselves to hell. *Exeunt.*

[II.iii] *Enter* Romelio, Ariosto.

ARIOSTO.
Your losses, I confess, are infinite,
Yet, sir, you must have patience.

ROMELIO.
Sir, my losses I know, but you I do not.

ARIOSTO.
'Tis most true,
I am but a stranger to you; but am wish'd
By some of your best friends to visit you,
And, out of my experience in the world,
To instruct you patience.

ROMELIO.
Of what profession are you?

ARIOSTO.
Sir, I am a lawyer.

ROMELIO.
Of all men living,
You lawyers I account the only men
To confirm patience in us: your delays
Would make three parts of this little Christian world
Run out of their wits else.
Now I remember you read lectures to Julio;
Are you such a leech for patience?

ARIOSTO.
Yes, sir, I have had some crosses.

4–6.] *Dyce;* Tis . . . am/ Wisht . . . you *Q*.

17. *leech for patience*] i.e., doctor (*leech*) who cures by administering patience.

ROMELIO.
You are married, then, I am certain.

ARIOSTO.
That I am, sir.

ROMELIO.
And have you studied patience?

ARIOSTO.
You shall find I have.

ROMELIO.
Did you ever see your wife make you cuckold?

ARIOSTO.
Make me a cuckold?

ROMELIO.
I ask it seriously. And you have not seen that,
Your patience has not ta'en the right degree
Of wearing scarlet; I should rather take you
For a bachelor in the art, than for a doctor.

ARIOSTO.
You are merry.

ROMELIO.
No, sir, with leave of your patience, I am horrible angry.

ARIOSTO.
What should move you
Put forth that harsh interrogatory, if these eyes
Ever saw my wife do the thing you wot of?

ROMELIO.
Why, I'll tell you:
Most radically to try your patience,
And the mere question shows you but a dunce in't.
It has made you angry: there's another lawyer's beard
In your forehead, you do bristle.

ARIOSTO.
You are very conceited.
But come, this is not the right way to cure you:
I must talk to you like a divine.

---

25. *And*] if.
27. *scarlet*] the color of robes for higher degrees at the university.
33. *wot*] know.
39. *conceited*] full of jests or conceits.

ROMELIO.

I have heard
Some talk of it very much, and many times
To their auditors' impatience; but I pray,
What practice do they make of't in their lives?
They are too full of choler with living honest,
And some of them not only impatient
Of their own slightest injuries, but stark mad
At one another's preferment. Now to you, sir:
I have lost three goodly carracks.

ARIOSTO.

So I hear.

ROMELIO. The very spice in them,
Had they been shipwrack'd here upon our coast,
Would have made all our sea a drench.

ARIOSTO.

All the sick horses in Italy
Would have been glad of your loss then.

ROMELIO.

You are conceited, too.

ARIOSTO.

Come, come, come,
You gave those ships most strange, most dreadful, and
Unfortunate names; I never look'd they'd prosper.

ROMELIO.

Is there any ill omen in giving names to ships?

ARIOSTO.

Did you not call one *The Storm's Defiance*,
Another, *The Scourge of the Sea*, and the third, *The Great*
Leviathan?

42–44.] *Dyce; prose in Q.*
58–59.] *Lucas;* You . . . dreadfull,/ And . . . prosper *Q.*
62–63.] *Lucas;* Another . . . third,/ The . . . Leuiathan *Q.*

---

46. *choler*] bile, the humor which supposedly caused bad temper.

50. *carracks*] large merchant ships.

53. *drench*] a drink, often medicinal, frequently made with spices.

58–67. *You . . . cradles*] Easy notes a parallel passage in Sir Robert Hawkins' *Voyage into the South Sea* (1622) about ominous naming of ships.

63. *Leviathan*] originally, a sea monster that often symbolized evil in Biblical literature.

ROMELIO.
Very right, sir.

ARIOSTO.
Very devilish names
All three of them; and surely I think
They were curs'd in their very cradles—I do mean,
When they were upon their stocks.

ROMELIO.
Come, you are superstitious,
I'll give you my opinion, and 'tis serious:
I am persuaded there came not cuckolds enow
To the first launching of them, and 'twas that
Made them thrive the worse for't. O,
Your cuckold's handsel is pray'd for i'th' City!

ARIOSTO.
I will hear no more.
Give me thy hand: my intent of coming hither
Was to persuade you to patience. As I live,
If ever I do visit you again,
It shall be to entreat you to be angry; sure I will,
I'll be as good as my word, believe it. *Exit* [Ariosto].

ROMELIO.
So, sir.

Enter Leonora.

How now?
Are the screech owls abroad already?

LEONORA.
What a dismal noise yon bell makes!
Sure some great person's dead.

72–74.] *this edn.;* To . . . them,/ And . . . for't./ Oh . . . Citie *Q*.

67, 68. *cradles, stocks*] framework in which a ship rests during construction. Ariosto seems for a moment to be thinking of an actual child in its cradle.

71. *enow*] enough.

74. *handsel*] The first money taken by a trader in the morning, it was considered lucky and from a cuckold supposedly brought great good fortune.

82. *screech owls*] In popular superstition, their cries presaged death.

83, 86. *bell, bellman*] A hand bell was rung by criers of news. Here, it probably rings slowly to suggest a death knell.

ROMELIO.

No such matter;
It is the common bellman goes about
To publish the sale of goods.

LEONORA.

Why do they ring before my gate thus?
Let them into th' court; I cannot understand
What they say.

Enter Two Bellmen and a Capuchin.

CAPUCHIN.

For pity's sake, you that have tears to shed,
Sigh a soft requiem, and let fall a bead
For two unfortunate nobles, whose sad fate
Leaves them both dead and excommunicate:
No churchman's prayer to comfort their last groans,
No sacred seed of earth to hide their bones;
But as their fury wrought them out of breath,
The canon speaks them guilty of their own death.

LEONORA.

What noble men, I pray, sir?

CAPUCHIN.

The Lord Ercole and the noble Contarino,
Both of them slain in single combat.

LEONORA.

O, I am lost forever!

ROMELIO.

Denied Christian burial! I pray, what does that,
Or the dead lazy march in the funeral,
Or the flattery in the epitaphs, which shows
More sluttish far than all the spiders' webs
Shall ever grow upon it—what do these
Add to our well-being after death?

---

92. *bead*] There is a double meaning of "a tear" and, more important, a prayer for the soul of the dead, or the rosary bead that represents that prayer.

96. *seed*] sod (Dyce), or merely small particles strewn about?

98. *canon*] church law.

104. *lazy*] slow-moving.

106. *sluttish*] dirty as well as low.

CAPUCHIN.

Not a scruple.

ROMELIO.

Very well then,
I have a certain meditation,
If I can think of't, somewhat to this purpose:
I'll say it to you, while my mother there
Numbers her beads.
You that dwell near these graves and vaults,
Which oft do hide physicians' faults,
Note what a small room does suffice,
To express men's good; their vanities
Would fill more volume in small hand
Than all the evidence of church-land.
Funerals hide men in civil wearing,
And are to the drapers a good hearing,
Make the heralds laugh in their black raiment,
And all die worthies, die worth payment
To the altar offerings, though their fame,
And all the charity of their name,
'Tween heaven and this yield no more light
Than rotten trees which shine i'th' night.
O, look the last act be the best i'th' play,
And then rest, gentle bones; yet pray
That when by the precise you are viewed,
A supersedeas be not sued,
To remove you to a place more airy,
That in your stead they may keep chary
Stockfish or seacoal, for the abuses
Of sacrilege have turn'd graves to vilder uses.

112. of't, somewhat] *Dyce;* of somewhat *Q*.

---

121. *civil wearing*] clothes befitting a citizen.

122. *good hearing*] good news.

124–125. *die worth . . . offerings*] who die worthy of having offerings made in their names.

132. *supersedeas*] a writ halting legal proceedings which ought otherwise to go forward, often under another writ. Here, an interruption.

134. *chary*] charily, carefully.

135. *Stockfish*] dried fish, generally cod.

135. *seacoal*] small coal washed ashore or freighted in by sea.

How then can any monument say,
Here rest these bones till the last day,
When time swift both of foot and feather,
May bear them the sexton kens not whither.
What care I, then, though my last sleep
Be in the desert or in the deep,
No lamp nor taper, day and night,
To give my charnel chargeable light?
I have there like quantity of ground,
And at the last day I shall be found.
Now I pray leave me.

CAPUCHIN.

I am sorry for your losses.

ROMELIO.

Um, sir, the more spacious that the tennis court is,
The more large is the hazard.
I dare the spiteful Fortune do her worst;
I can now fear nothing.

CAPUCHIN.

O, sir, yet consider,
He that is without fear, is without hope,
And sins from presumption; better thoughts attend you.

Exeunt Capuchin [*and Bellmen*].

ROMELIO.

Poor Jolenta! Should she hear of this,
She would not after the report keep fresh
So long as flowers in graves.

Enter Prospero.

How now, Prospero?

PROSPERO.

Contarino has sent you here his will,
Wherein 'a has made your sister his sole heir.

ROMELIO.

Is he not dead?

155.1.] *Dyce; Exit* Capuchin *at l. 156 in Q.*

158.] *Dyce;* So . . . graues./ How . . . *Prospero Q.*

144. *chargeable*] expensive.

150. *hazard*] in indoor court tennis, one of three openings in the walls through which the ball may be hit to score points.

PROSPERO.
He's yet living.

ROMELIO.
Living? The worse luck!

LEONORA.
The worse? I do protest it is the best
That ever came to disturb my prayers.

ROMELIO.
How?

LEONORA.
Yet I would have him live
To satisfy public justice for the death
Of Ercole. O, go visit him for heaven's sake!
I have within my closet a choice relic,
Preservative 'gainst swounding, and some earth
Brought from the Holy Land, right sovereign
To staunch blood. Has he skillful surgeons, think you?

PROSPERO.
The best in Naples.

ROMELIO.
How oft has he been drest?

PROSPERO.
But once.

LEONORA.
I have some skill this way:
The second or third dressing will show clearly
Whether there be hope of life. I pray, be near him;
If there be any soul can bring me word
That there is hope of life—

ROMELIO.
Do you prize his life so?

LEONORA.
That he may live, I mean,
To come to his trial, to satisfy the law.

ROMELIO.
O, is't nothing else?

LEONORA.
I shall be the happiest woman!

Exeunt Leonora, Prospero.

182–183.] *Dyce;* That . . . liue;/ I . . . Law *Q*.

ROMELIO.

Here is cruelty appareled in kindness!
I am full of thoughts, strange ones, but they're no good ones.
I must visit Contarino; upon that
Depends an engine shall weigh up my losses,
Were they sunk as low as hell. Yet let me think
How I am impaired in an hour, and the cause of't,
Lost in security; O, how this wicked world bewitches,
Especially made insolent with riches!
So sails with fore-winds stretch'd do soonest break,
And pyramids o'th' top are still most weak. *Exit.*

[II.iv] *Enter* Capuchin, Ercole *led between two.*

CAPUCHIN.

Look up, sir. You are preserved beyond natural reason; you were brought dead out o'th' field, the surgeons ready to have embalmed you.

ERCOLE.

I do look on my action with a thought of terror;
To do ill and dwell in't, is unmanly.

CAPUCHIN.

You are divinely informed, sir.

ERCOLE.

I fought for one in whom I have no more right
Than false executors have in orphans' goods
They cozen them of; yet though my cause were naught,
I rather chose the hazard of my soul,
Than forgo the complement of a choleric man.
I pray, continue the report of my death, and give out,

191. an] *Dyce;* a *Q*.

[II.iv]
11. forgo] *Dyce;* foregoe *Q*.

---

189. *engine*] device (here used figuratively).
189. *weigh up*] restore; actually, to raise, as one weighs anchor.
191. *am impaired*] have suffered loss.
194. *fore-winds*] "wind that blows a ship forward on her course" (*OED*).

[II.iv]
5. *dwell*] continue.
6. *informed*] guided.
9. *cozen*] cheat.
11. *complement*] reputation.

'Cause the Church denied me Christian burial,
The vice-admiral of my galleys took my body,
With purpose to commit it to the earth,
Either in Sicil or Malta.

CAPUCHIN.
What aim you at by this rumor of your death?

ERCOLE.
There is hope of life
In Contarino, and he has my prayers
That he may live to enjoy what is his own,
The fair Jolenta; where, should it be thought
That I were breathing, happily her friends
Would oppose it still.

CAPUCHIN.
But if you be supposed dead,
The law will strictly prosecute his life
For your murder.

ERCOLE. That's prevented thus:
There does belong a noble privilege
To all his family, ever since his father
Bore from the worthy Emperor, Charles the Fifth,
An answer to the French King's challenge, at such time
The two noble princes were engag'd to fight,
Upon a frontier arm o'th' sea in a flat-bottom'd boat,
That if any of his family should chance
To kill a man i'th' field in a noble cause,
He should have his pardon. Now, sir, for his cause,
The world may judge if it were not honest.
Pray help me in speech, 'tis very painful to me.

CAPUCHIN.
Sir, I shall.

ERCOLE.
The guilt of this lies in Romelio;
And as I hear, to second this good contract,
He has got a nun with child.

16. Sicil] *Dyce;* Cicil *Q.*

---

21. *where*] whereas.
29–32. *Emperor . . . boat*] in 1528, Charles V of Spain and Francis I of France exchanged various challenges, and Charles later spoke of one to fight hand-to-hand in a boat (Lucas).

CAPUCHIN.

These are crimes that either must make work
For speedy repentance or for the devil.

ERCOLE.

I have much compassion on him,
For sin and shame are ever tied together
With Gordian knots, of such a strong thread spun,
They cannot without violence be undone. *Exeunt.*

Explicit Actus Secundus.

[III.i] *Enter* Ariosto, Crispiano.

ARIOSTO.

Well sir, now I must claim
Your promise, to reveal to me the cause
Why you live thus clouded.

CRISPIANO.

Sir, the King of Spain
Suspects that your Romelio here, the merchant,
Has discover'd some gold mine to his own use,
In the West Indies, and for that employs me
To discover in what part of Christendom
He vents this treasure; besides, he is informed
What mad tricks has been play'd of late by ladies.

ARIOSTO.

Most true, and I am glad the King has heard on't.
Why, they use their lords as if they were their wards;
And as your Dutchwomen in the Low Countries

1–3.] *Dyce;* Well . . . promise,/ To . . . clouded *Q.*

46–47. *Gordian knots . . . undone*] Gordius, King of Phrygia, tied a knot impossible to loose. Alexander the Great cut it and, fulfilling an attendant prophecy, became ruler of Asia.

[III.i]

3. *clouded*] obscured, i.e., disguised.

9. *vents*] has an outlet for.

13–18]. Dutch wives were notorious for domineering over husbands chosen for their simplicity (Lucas quotes from Fynes Moryson, *Itinerary*, Pt. III, Bk. 4, Ch. 6).

Take all and pay all, and do keep their husbands
So silly all their lives of their own estates
That, when they are sick and come to make their will,
They know not precisely what to give away
From their wives, because they know not what they are worth,
So here should I repeat what factions,
What bat-fowling for offices—
As you must conceive their game is all i'th' night—
What calling in question one another's honesties,
Withal what sway they bear i'th' Viceroy's court,
You'd wonder at it.
'Twill do well, shortly, can we keep them off
From being of our council of war.

CRISPIANO.
Well, I have vowed
That I will never sit upon the bench more,
Unless it be to curb the insolencies
Of these women.

ARIOSTO.
Well, take it on my word, then,
Your place will not long be empty. *Exeunt.*

[III.ii] *Enter* Romelio *in the habit of a Jew.*

ROMELIO.
Excellently well habited! Why, methinks
That I could play with mine own shadow now,
And be a rare Italianated Jew;

---

14. *Take all and pay all*] an idiom for ruling over household business.

15. *silly*] ignorant.

20. *bat-fowling*] catching birds at night, using a light to daze them before knocking them from their perches; also Elizabethan slang for any unfair advantage.

21. *conceive*] keep in mind.

[III.ii]

0.1.] Traditional stage disguise for a Jew would include a large false nose and a gaberdine (a coarse, loose-fitting gown).

3. *Italianated Jew*] Webster's audience might think of Marlowe's Machiavellian Barabas in *Jew of Malta*, and betraying a town (l. 13) seems a specific allusion.

To have as many several change of faces
As I have seen carv'd upon one cherry stone;
To wind about a man like rotten ivy,
Eat into him like quicksilver, poison a friend
With pulling but a loose hair from's beard, or give a drench,
He should linger of't nine years, and ne'er complain
But in the spring and fall, and so the cause
Imputed to the disease natural; for slight villainies,
As to coin money, corrupt ladies' honors,
Betray a town to th' Turk, or make a bonfire
O'th' Christian navy, I could settle to't,
As if I had eat a politician
And disgested him to nothing but pure blood.
But stay, I lose myself: this is the house.
Within there! [*He knocks.*]

Enter Two Surgeons.

FIRST SURGEON.
Now, sir?

ROMELIO.
You are the men of art that, as I hear,
Have the Lord Contarino under cure.

SECOND SURGEON.
Yes, sir, we are his surgeons,
But he is past all cure.

ROMELIO. Why, is he dead?

FIRST SURGEON.
He is speechless, sir, and we do find his wound
So fester'd near the vitals, all our art
By warm drinks cannot clear th'impostumation,

5. one] *Dyce;* on *Q.*
18. S.D. *He knocks*] *Lucas.*

4–14.] a sampling of what early seventeenth-century Englishmen considered typical Italian villainy.

4. *several*] different.

7. *quicksilver*] mercury, poisonous if gotten into the mouth, and capable of dissolving other metals such as gold.

16. *disgested*] digested.

26. *impostumation*] abscess.

And he's so weak, to make incision
By the orifix were present death to him.

ROMELIO.
He has made a will, I hear.

FIRST SURGEON. Yes, sir.

ROMELIO.
And deputed Jolenta his heir.

SECOND SURGEON.
He has, we are witness to't.

ROMELIO.
Has not Romelio been with you yet,
To give you thanks and ample recompense
For the pains you have ta'en?

FIRST SURGEON.
Not yet.

ROMELIO.
Listen to me, gentlemen, for I protest,
If you will seriously mind your own good,
I am come about a business shall convey
Large legacies from Contarino's will
To both of you.

SECOND SURGEON.
How, sir? Why, Romelio has the will,
And in that he has given us nothing.

ROMELIO.
I pray, attend me: I am a physician.

SECOND SURGEON.
A physician? Where do you practice?

ROMELIO.
In Rome.

FIRST SURGEON. O, then you have store of patients.

ROMELIO.
Store! Why, look you, I can kill my twenty a month
And work but i'th' forenoons—you will give me leave

27. incision] *Dyce; omitted in Q.*
41–42.] *Dyce;* How Sir?/ Why . . .
nothing *Q.*

28. *orifix*] orifice, opening.
45. *store of patients*] "owing to the abundant crime and vice in Rome" (Lucas).

To jest and be merry with you. —But as I said,
All my study has been physic; I am sent
From a noble Roman that is near akin
To Contarino, and that ought indeed,
By the law of alliance, be his only heir,
To practice his good and yours.

BOTH. How, I pray, sir?

ROMELIO.

I can by an extraction which I have,
Though he were speechless, his eyes set in's head,
His pulses without motion, restore to him,
For half an hour's space, the use of sense,
And perhaps a little speech; having done this,
If we can work him, as no doubt we shall,
To make another will, and therein assign
This gentleman his heir, I will assure you,
'Fore I depart this house, ten thousand ducats;
And then we'll pull the pillow from his head,
And let him e'en go whither the religion sends him
That he died in.

FIRST SURGEON.

Will you give's ten thousand ducats?

ROMELIO.

Upon my Jewism.

SECOND SURGEON.

'Tis a bargain, sir; we are yours.

Contarino [*discovered*] *in a bed.*

Here is the subject you must work on.

ROMELIO.

Well said; you are honest men,
And go to the business roundly: but, gentlemen,
I must use my art singly.

FIRST SURGEON.

O, sir, you shall have all privacy.

ROMELIO.

And the doors lock'd to me.

---

54. *extraction*] extract, presumably from medicinal herbs.

68.1.] Either the curtain of an inner stage was opened, or a bed was thrust forward onto the stage for the discovery (Dyce).

SECOND SURGEON.

At your best pleasure.
[*Aside.*] Yet for all this, I will not trust this Jew.

FIRST SURGEON [*aside*].

Faith, to say truth,
I do not like him neither; he looks like a rogue.
This is a fine toy, fetch a man to life,
To make a new will! There's some trick in't.
I'll be near you, Jew. *Exeunt* Surgeons.

ROMELIO.

Excellent as I would wish: these credulous fools
Have given me freely what I would have bought
With a great deal of money. —Softly, here's breath yet.
Now, Ercole, for part of the revenge
Which I have vow'd for thy untimely death,
Besides this politic working of my own,
That scorns precedent. Why, should this great man live
And not enjoy my sister—as I have vowed
He never shall—O, he may alter's will
Every new moon if he please; to prevent which,
I must put in a strong caveat. Come forth, then,
My desperate stiletto, that may be worn
In a woman's hair, and ne'er discover'd,
And either would be taken for a bodkin,
Or a curling iron at most; why, 'tis an engine
That's only fit to put in execution
Barmotho pigs, a most unmanly weapon,
That steals into a man's life he knows not how.
O great Caesar, he that past the shock
Of so many armed pikes, and poison'd darts,
Swords, slings, and battleaxes, should at length,
Sitting at ease on a cushion, come to die

76. S.D.] *Lucas.*
77. S.D.] *Lucas.*
90. shall—] *this edn.;* shall? *Q.*
97–98.] *Dyce;* That's . . . Pigs,/ A . . . weapon *Q.*

92. *caveat*] legal notice stopping some procedure until the opposition has been heard.

93. *desperate*] suitable for use in the last extremity.

95. *bodkin*] a long hairpin.

98. *Barmotho*] Bermuda, known in Webster's time for numerous hogs.

By such a shoemaker's awl as this, his soul let forth
At a hole no bigger than the incision
Made for a wheal! Ud's foot, I am horribly angry
That he should die so scurvily: yet wherefore
Do I condemn thee thereof so cruelly,
Yet shake him by the hand? 'Tis to express
That I would never have such weapons used
But in a plot like this, that's treacherous.
Yet this shall prove most merciful to thee,
For it shall preserve thee
From dying on a public scaffold, and withal
Bring thee an absolute cure, thus. *Stabs him.*
So, 'tis done; and now for my escape.

Enter Surgeons.

FIRST SURGEON.
You rogue mountebank,
I will try whether your inwards can endure
To be wash'd in scalding lead.

ROMELIO.
Hold, I turn Christian.

SECOND SURGEON.
Nay, prithee, be a Jew still;
I would not have a Christian be guilty
Of such a villainous act as this is.

ROMELIO.
I am Romelio the merchant.

FIRST SURGEON.
Romelio! You have proved yourself
A cunning merchant indeed.

ROMELIO.
You may read why I came hither.

---

106. *wheal*] blister.
106. *Ud's foot*] a strong oath, "by God's foot," i.e., the foot of Christ.
108. *thee*] the dagger.
119. *wash'd . . . lead*] evidently a form of torture or trial by ordeal; ability to endure extreme heat was proof of righteousness.
120. *turn Christian*] often a way to escape the worst punishments.

SECOND SURGEON.

Yes, in a bloody Roman letter.

ROMELIO.

I did hate this man; each minute of his breath
Was torture to me.

FIRST SURGEON.

Had you forborne this act, he had not liv'd
This two hours.

ROMELIO.

But he had died then,
And my revenge unsatisfied. Here's gold;
Never did wealthy man purchase the silence
Of a terrible scolding wife at a dearer rate
Than I will pay for yours: here's your earnest
In a bag of double ducats.

SECOND SURGEON.

Why look you, sir, as I do weigh this business,
This cannot be counted murder in you by no means.
Why, 'tis no more than should I go and choke
An Irishman, that were three quarters drown'd
With pouring usquebaugh in's throat.

ROMELIO.

You will be secret?

FIRST SURGEON.

As your soul.

ROMELIO.

The West Indies shall sooner want gold than you, then.

SECOND SURGEON.

That protestation has the music of the mint in't.

ROMELIO [*aside*].

How unfortunately was I surpris'd! I have made myself a slave perpetually to these two beggars. *Exit.*

143. usquebaugh] *Dyce;* Vsquebath Q. 148. S.D.] *Dyce.*

---

128. *Roman letter*] a reference to the Roman script, a round, bold hand (*OED*) and Romelio's pretending to be from Rome.

137. *earnest*] part payment, "especially for the purpose of binding a bargain" (*OED*).

143. *usquebaugh*] whiskey.

FIRST SURGEON.
Excellent; by this act he has made his estate ours.

SECOND SURGEON.
I'll presently grow a lazy surgeon, and ride on my footcloth. I'll fetch from him every eight days a policy for a hundred double ducats; if he grumble, I'll peach.

FIRST SURGEON.
But let's take heed he do not poison us.

SECOND SURGEON.
O, I will never eat nor drink with him,
Without unicorn's horn in a hollow tooth.

CONTARINO.
O!

FIRST SURGEON.
Did he not groan?

SECOND SURGEON. Is the wind in that door still?

FIRST SURGEON.
Ha! Come hither, note a strange accident:
His steel has lighted in the former wound,
And made free passage for the congealed blood.
Observe in what abundance it delivers the putrefaction.

SECOND SURGEON.
Methinks he fetches his breath very lively.

FIRST SURGEON.
The hand of heaven is in't,
That his intent to kill him should become
The very direct way to save his life.

SECOND SURGEON.
Why, this is like one I have heard of in England,
Was cured o'th' gout by being rack'd i'th' Tower.
Well, if we can recover him, here's reward
On both sides. Howsoever, we must be secret.

---

152. *policy*] bond (Lucas).
153. *peach*] turn informer.
156. *unicorn's horn . . . tooth*] a supposed antidote for poison.
158. *Is . . . still*] are things still that way, i.e., is he still alive?
168. *cured . . . Tower*] evidently a topical allusion, for it is also used by Jonson (*Volpone*, ed. Spencer, IV.vi.33) and Marston (*Malcontent*, ed. Spencer, III.i.88–90).
168. *rack'd*] stretched on the rack.
169. *recover*] cure.

FIRST SURGEON.

We are tied to't:
When we cure gentlemen of foul diseases,
They give us so much for the cure, and twice as much
That we do not blab on't. Come, let's to work roundly;
Heat the lotion and bring the searing. *Exeunt.*

[III.iii]

A table set forth with two tapers, a death's head, a book. Jolenta *in mourning*; Romelio *sits by her.*

ROMELIO.

Why do you grieve thus? Take a looking glass,
And see if this sorrow become you; that pale face
Will make men think you us'd some art before,
Some odious painting. Contarino's dead.

JOLENTA.

O, that he should die so soon!

ROMELIO.

Why, I pray tell me,
Is not the shortest fever the best, and are not bad plays
The worse for their length?

JOLENTA.

Add not to th'ill y'ave done
An odious slander; he stuck i'th'eyes o'th' court
As the most choice jewel there.

ROMELIO.

O, be not angry!
Indeed the court to well-composed nature
Adds much to perfection; for it is, or should be,
As a bright crystal mirror to the world,
To dress itself. But I must tell you, sister,
If th'excellency of the place could have wrought salvation,
The devil had ne'er fall'n from heaven; he was proud.

[Jolenta *rises.*]

Leave us, leave us?
Come, take your seat again; I have a plot,
If you will listen to it seriously,

175. *searing*] usually "searing-iron," a cauterizing iron (*OED*).

That goes beyond example; it shall breed,
Out of the death of these two noble men,
The advancement of our house.

JOLENTA.

O take heed! A grave is a rotten foundation.

ROMELIO.

Nay, nay, hear me.
'Tis somewhat indirectly, I confess;
But there is much advancement in the world
That comes in indirectly. I pray mind me:
You are already made by absolute will
Contarino's heir; now, if it can be proved
That you have issue by Lord Ercole,
I will make you inherit his land too.

JOLENTA.

How's this?
Issue by him, he dead, and I a virgin?

ROMELIO.

I know you would wonder how it could be done,
But I have laid the case so radically,
Not all the lawyers in Christendom
Shall find any the least flaw in't. I have a mistress
Of the Order of Saint Clare, a beauteous nun,
Who being cloister'd ere she knew the heat
Her blood would arrive to, had only time enough
To repent, and idleness sufficient
To fall in love with me; and to be short,
I have so much disordered the holy order,
I have got this nun with child.

JOLENTA.

Excellent work made for a dumb midwife.

ROMELIO.

I am glad you grow thus pleasant.
Now will I have you presently give out
That you are full two months quicken'd with child

34–35.] *Dyce; one line in Q.*

---

37. *radically*] carefully, i.e., from the roots up.

40. *Order of Saint Clare*] the Poor Ladies, or Clares; the order was founded by St. Francis of Assisi and St. Clare.

By Ercole, which rumor can beget
No scandal to you, since we will affirm
The precontract was so exactly done,
By the same words used in the form of marriage,
That with a little dispensation,
A money matter, it shall be register'd
Absolute matrimony.

JOLENTA.
So. Then I conceive you,
My conceived child must prove your bastard.

ROMELIO.
Right;
For at such time my mistress falls in labor,
You must feign the like.

JOLENTA.
'Tis a pretty feat, this,
But I am not capable of it.

ROMELIO. Not capable?

JOLENTA.
No, for the thing you would have me counterfeit
Is most essentially put in practice, nay, 'tis done:
I am with child already.

ROMELIO. Ha! By whom?

JOLENTA.
By Contarino. Do not knit the brow;
The precontract shall justify it, it shall;
Nay, I will get some singular fine churchman,
Or though he be a plural one, shall affirm
He coupled us together.

ROMELIO. O misfortune!
Your child must then be reputed Ercole's.

60–64. Right . . . it] *Dyce;* Right . . . time/ My . . . like./ Tis . . . it *Q*.

---

53. *precontract*] civil betrothal agreement. It had to be followed by a church ceremony to make a marriage valid.

58. *conceive*] understand.

70. *singular*] singularly, with a bit of word play in the contrast to *plural* (l. 71).

71. *plural*] holding more than one benefice at a time, a reprehensible practice.

JOLENTA.

Your hopes are dash'd, then, since your votary's issue
Must not inherit the land.

ROMELIO. No matter for that,
So I preserve her fame. I am strangely puzzled:
Why, suppose that she be brought abed before you,
And we conceal her issue till the time
Of your delivery, and then give out
That you have two at a birth; ha, were't not excellent?

JOLENTA.

And what resemblance, think you, would they have
To one another? Twins are still alike.
But this is not your aim; you would have your child
Inherit Ercole's land. O my sad soul!
Have you not made me yet wretched enough,
But after all this frosty age in youth,
Which you have witch'd upon me, you will seek
To poison my fame?

ROMELIO.

That's done already.

JOLENTA.

No, sir, I did but feign it,
To a fatal purpose, as I thought.

ROMELIO.

What purpose?

JOLENTA.

If you had lov'd or tender'd my dear honor,
You would have lock'd your poniard in my heart
When I nam'd I was with child; but I must live
To linger out, till the consumption
Of my own sorrow kill me.

ROMELIO [*aside*]. This will not do;
The devil has on the sudden furnish'd me
With a rare charm, yet a most unnatural falsehood:

96–97. To . . . me] *Dyce;* To . . . owne/ Sorrow kill me *Q*.
97. S.D.] *Dyce*.
97–100. This . . . take] *Lucas; prose in Q*.

74. *votary's*] nun's.
76. *fame*] reputation.
82. *still*] always.

No matter, so 'twill take.—
Stay, sister, I would utter to you a business,
But I am very loath: a thing, indeed,
Nature would have compassionately conceal'd
Till my mother's eyes be closed.

JOLENTA.
Pray, what's that, sir?

ROMELIO.
You did observe
With what a dear regard our mother tender'd
The Lord Contarino, yet how passionately
She sought to cross the match: why, this was merely
To blind the eye o'th' world; for she did know
That you would marry him, and he was capable.
My mother doted upon him, and it was plotted
Cunningly between them, after you were married,
Living all three together in one house—
A thing I cannot whisper without horror—
Why, the malice scarce of devils would suggest
Incontinence 'tween them two.

JOLENTA.
I remember since his hurt,
She has been very passionately inquiring
After his health.

ROMELIO. Upon my soul, this jewel,
With a piece of the holy cross in't, this relic,
Valued at many thousand crowns,
She would have sent him, lying upon his deathbed.

JOLENTA.
Professing, as you say,
Love to my mother, wherefore did he make
Me his heir?

ROMELIO.
His will was made afore he went to fight,
When he was first a suitor to you.

122–123.] *this edn.; prose in Q.*

---

107. *tender'd*] treated.
116. *malice . . . suggest*] the malice of devils would scarcely suggest.

JOLENTA.
To fight! O, well remember'd:
If he lov'd my mother, wherefore did he lose
His life in my quarrel?

ROMELIO.
For the affront sake, a word you understand not:
Because Ercole was pretended rival to him,
To clear your suspicion. I was gull'd in't too.
Should he not have fought upon't,
He had undergone the censure of a coward.

JOLENTA.
How came you by this wretched knowledge?

ROMELIO.
His surgeon overheard it,
As he did sigh it out to his confessor,
Some half hour 'fore he died.

JOLENTA.
I would have the surgeon hang'd
For abusing confession, and for making me
So wretched by th' report. Can this be truth?

ROMELIO.
No, but direct falsehood
As ever was banish'd the court. Did you ever hear
Of a mother that has kept her daughter's husband
For her own tooth? He fancied you in one kind,
For his lust, and he loved
Our mother in another kind, for her money;
The gallant's fashion right. But come, ne'er think on't;
Throw the fowl to the devil that hatch'd it, and let this
Bury all ill that's in't: she is our mother.

JOLENTA.
I never did find anything i'th' world
Turn my blood so much as this: here's such a conflict
Between apparent presumption and unbelief

150. gallant's] *Dyce;* Gallants *Q.*

---

134. *To . . . suspicion*] to allay your suspicion that he did not love you.
136. *undergone the censure*] suffered the reputation.
144. *direct falsehood*] complete treachery (referring to Contarino's "plot").
151. *fowl*] with a secondary meaning of "foul."
155. *apparent*] obvious.

That I shall die in't.
O, if there be another world i'th' moon,
As some fantastics dream, I could wish all men,
The whole race of them, for their inconstancy
Sent thither to people that. Why, I protest,
I now affect the Lord Ercole's memory
Better than the other's.

ROMELIO.
But were Contarino living?

JOLENTA.
I do call anything to witness
That the divine law prescribed us
To strengthen an oath, were he living and in health,
I would never marry with him.
Nay, since I have found the world
So false to me, I'll be as false to it;
I will mother this child for you.

ROMELIO.
Hah?

JOLENTA.
Most certainly it will beguile part of my sorrow.

ROMELIO.
O, most assuredly; make you smile to think
How many times i'th' world lordships descend
To divers men, that might, and truth were known,
Be heir, for anything belongs to'th' flesh,
As well to the Turk's richest eunuch.

JOLENTA.
But do you not think
I shall have a horrible strong breath now?

ROMELIO.
Why?

JOLENTA.
O, with keeping your counsel, 'tis so terrible foul.

ROMELIO.
Come, come, come,
You must leave these bitter flashes.

157–158. *if . . . dream*] Galileo and others were observing mountains and valleys on the moon. Dyce cites a similar line in *Paradise Lost*, III, 459.

174. *and*] if.

JOLENTA.
Must I dissemble dishonesty? You have divers
Counterfeit honesty: but I hope here's none
Will take exceptions; I now must practice
The art of a great-bellied woman, and go feign
Their qualms and swoundings.

ROMELIO.
Eat unripe fruit and oatmeal, to take away your color.

JOLENTA.
Dine in my bed some two hours after noon.

ROMELIO.
And when you are up,
Make to your petticoat a quilted preface,
To advance your belly.

JOLENTA.
I have a strange conceit now.
I have known some women, when they were with child,
Have long'd to beat their husbands: what if I,
To keep decorum, exercise my longing
Upon my tailor that way, and noddle him soundly?
He'll make the larger bill for't.

ROMELIO.
I'll get one shall be as tractable to't as stockfish.

JOLENTA.
O, my fantastical sorrow! Cannot I now
Be miserable enough, unless I wear
A pied fool's coat! Nay worse, for when our passions
Such giddy and uncertain changes breed,
We are never well, till we are mad indeed. *Exit.*

200–202.] *Dyce*; Oh . . . sorrow,/ Cannot . . . enough,/ Vnlesse . . . coat:/Nay . . . passions *Q*.

---

187. *qualms*] sudden fits of illness or faintness and swooning.

191. *preface*] front.

193. *conceit*] whim.

196. *keep decorum*] behave appropriately.

197. *noddle*] beat about the head and back of the neck.

199. *tractable . . . stockfish*] The air-dried cod were beaten before being cooked.

ROMELIO.

So. Nothing in the world could have done this,
But to beget in her a strong distaste
Of the Lord Contarino. O jealousy,
How violent, especially in women!
How often has it rais'd the devil up
In form of a law-case! My especial care
Must be, to nourish craftily this fiend
'Tween the mother and the daughter, that the deceit
Be not perceived. My next task, that my sister,
After this supposed childbirth, be persuaded
To enter into religion: 'tis concluded
She must never marry; so I am left guardian
To her estate. And lastly, that my two surgeons
Be waged to the East Indies: let them prate
When they are beyond the line; the calenture,
Or the scurvy, or the Indian pox, I hope,
Will take order for their coming back.

Enter Leonora.

O, here's my mother. I ha' strange news for you:
My sister is with child.

LEONORA.

I do look now for some great misfortunes
To follow, for indeed, mischiefs
Are like the visits of Franciscan friars:
They never come to prey upon us single.
In what estate left you Contarino?

ROMELIO.

Strange that you can skip
From the former sorrow to such a question!
I'll tell you: in the absence of his surgeon,

209–211.] *Dyce;* How . . . case!/ My . . . fiend *Q*.

---

218. *waged*] hired to go.
219. *line*] the equator.
219. *calenture*] delirium-producing disease that made sailors in the tropics mistake the sea for green fields and try to jump overboard.
220. *Indian pox*] syphilis.
221. *take order for*] take measures against.
226–227. *visits . . . single*] Franciscans had to wander in pairs.

My charity did that for him in a trice,
They would have done at leisure and been paid for't:
I have killed him.

LEONORA.
I am twenty years elder since you last opened your lips.

ROMELIO.
Ha?

LEONORA.
You have given him the wound you speak of
Quite through your mother's heart.

ROMELIO.
I will heal it presently, mother, for this sorrow
Belongs to your error: you would have him live
Because you think he's father of the child;
But Jolenta vows by all the rights of truth,
'Tis Ercole's. It makes me smile to think
How cunningly my sister could be drawn
To the contract, and yet how familiarly
To his bed. Doves never couple
Without a kind of murmur.

LEONORA.
O, I am very sick!

ROMELIO.
Your old disease: when you are griev'd,
You are troubled with the mother.

LEONORA.
I am rapt with the mother indeed,
That I ever bore such a son.

ROMELIO.
Pray tend my sister;
I am infinitely full of business.

LEONORA.
Stay, you will mourn for Contarino?

ROMELIO.
O, by all means; 'tis fit—my sister is his heir. *Exit.*

---

244. *How . . . drawn*] how much cunning it took to lead her.
250. *mother*] hysteria.
251. *rapt*] carried away, perhaps with an overtone of being rapped or punished for motherhood.

LEONORA.
I will make you chief mourner, believe it.
Never was woe like mine. O, that my care
And absolute study to preserve his life
Should be his absolute ruin! Is he gone then?
There is no plague i'th' world can be compared
To impossible desire, for they are plagued
In the desire itself. Never, O never
Shall I behold him living, in whose life
I lived far sweetlier than in mine own.
A precise curiosity has undone me: why did I not
Make my love known directly? 'T had not been
Beyond example for a matron
To affect i'th' honorable way of marriage
So youthful a person. O, I shall run mad!
For as we love our youngest children best,
So the last fruit of our affection,
Wherever we bestow it, is most strong,
Most violent, most unresistable,
Since 'tis indeed our latest harvest-home,
Last merriment 'fore winter; and we widows,
As men report of our best picture-makers,
We love the piece we are in hand with better
Than all the excellent work we have done before.
And my son has depriv'd me of all this. Ha, my son!
I'll be a fury to him; like an Amazon lady,
I'd cut off this right pap, that gave him suck,
To shoot him dead. I'll no more tender him,
Than had a wolf stol'n to my teat i'th' night
And robb'd me of my milk; nay, such a creature
I should love better far. —Ha, ha, what say you?
I do talk to somewhat, methinks; it may be
My evil genius. Do not the bells ring?

282. this] *Q(corr.)*; his *Q(uncorr.)*.

262. *they*] those who desire.
266. *precise curiosity*] overly subtle behavior.
269. *affect*] seek after.
281–283. *like an Amazon . . . dead*] These warrior women reputedly had the right breast removed to facilitate drawing a bowstring.
283. *tender*] feel tenderly towards.

I have a strange noise in my head: O, fly in pieces!
Come, age, and wither me into the malice
Of those that have been happy; let me have
One property more than the devil of hell,
Let me envy the pleasure of youth heartily;
Let me in this life fear no kind of ill,
That have no good to hope for. Let me die
In the distraction of that worthy princess
Who loathed food, and sleep, and ceremony,
For thought of losing that brave gentleman
She would fain have saved, had not a false conveyance
Express'd him stubborn-hearted.
Let me sink where neither man
Nor memory may ever find me. *Falls down.*

[*Enter* Capuchin *and* Ercole.]

CAPUCHIN.
This is a private way which I command
As her confessor. I would not have you seen yet,
Till I prepare her. [Ercole *retires.*]
Peace to you, lady.

LEONORA.
Ha?

CAPUCHIN.
You are well employ'd, I hope. The best
Pillow i'th' world for this your contemplation
Is the earth, and the best object, heaven.

LEONORA.
I am whispering to a dead friend.

299. conveyance] *Q(corr.)*; countenance *Q(uncorr.)*.
300.] *Q(corr.)*; *omitted in Q(uncorr.)*.
302.1.] *Dyce.*
305. S.D.] *Dyce.*
307–309.] *this edn.;* You . . . i'th/ World . . . earth,/ And . . . heauen *Q*.

289. *fly in pieces*] like an old, overcharged cannon (Lucas).
296–300.] an early reference to the romanticized story of Queen Elizabeth's mourning for Essex's death. The Countess of Nottingham confessed she had not passed on a ring Essex had sent the Queen in suit for pardon, and had made him seem intransigent (Lucas).
299. *conveyance*] transmittal, with an overtone of furtive action.
300. *Express'd*] made him appear.

CAPUCHIN.
And I am come
To bring you tidings of a friend was dead,
Restored to life again.

LEONORA. Say, sir?

CAPUCHIN.
One whom I dare presume, next to your children,
You tender'd above life.

LEONORA.
Heaven will not suffer me utterly to be lost.

CAPUCHIN.
For he should have been
Your son-in-law, miraculously saved,
When surgery gave him o'er.

LEONORA. O, may you live
To win many souls to heaven, worthy sir,
That your crown may be the greater. Why, my son
Made me believe he stole into his chamber,
And ended that which Ercole began
By a deadly stab in's heart.

ERCOLE [*aside*]. Alas, she mistakes!
'Tis Contarino she wishes living; but I must fasten
On her last words, for my own safety.

LEONORA.
Where, O where shall I meet this comfort?

[Ercole *steps forward.*]

ERCOLE.
Here in the vowed comfort of your daughter.

LEONORA.
O, I am dead again! Instead of the man,
You present me the grave swallowed him.

ERCOLE.
Collect yourself, good lady.
Would you behold brave Contarino living?

312. was] *Q(corr.)*; not *Q(uncorr.)*.
313. Restored] *Q(corr.)*; Reserved *Q(uncorr.)*.
324. S.D.] *Dyce.*
329–330.] *Dyce; prose in Q.*

328. *vowed*] betrothed.
328. *comfort*] a misprint for "consort"? (Lucas).

There cannot be a nobler chronicle
Of his good than myself: if you would view him dead,
I will present him to you bleeding fresh,
In my penitency.

LEONORA. Sir, you do only live
To redeem another ill you have committed,
That my poor innocent daughter perish not
By your vild sin, whom you have got with child.

ERCOLE.
Here begin all my compassion. O poor soul!
She is with child by Contarino; and he dead,
By whom should she preserve her fame to'th' world
But by myself that loved her 'bove the world?
There never was a way more honorable
To exercise my virtue than to father it,
And preserve her credit, and to marry her.
I'll suppose her Contarino's widow, bequeath'd to me
Upon his death; for sure she was his wife,
But that the ceremony o'th' church was wanting.
Report this to her, Madam, and withal,
That never father did conceive more joy
For the birth of an heir, than I to understand
She had such confidence in me. I will not now
Press a visit upon her, till you have prepar'd her;
For I do read in your distraction,
Should I be brought o'th' sudden to her presence,
Either the hasty fright, or else the shame
May blast the fruit within her. I will leave you
To commend as loyal faith and service to her
As e'er heart harbor'd; by my hope of bliss,
I never liv'd to do good act but this.

CAPUCHIN [*aside to* Ercole].
Withal, and you be wise,
Remember what the mother has reveal'd
Of Romelio's treachery. *Exeunt* Ercole, Capuchin.

LEONORA.
A most noble fellow! In his loyalty
I read what worthy comforts I have lost

362. S.D.] *Dyce*. 365. fellow!] *Dyce;* fellow *Q*.

In my dear Contarino, and all adds
To my despair. —Within there!

Enter Winifrid.

Fetch the picture
Hangs in my inner closet. *Exit* Winifrid.
I remember
I let a word slip of Romelio's practice
At the surgeons'. No matter, I can salve it;
I have deeper vengeance that's preparing for him:
To let him live and kill him, that's revenge
I meditate upon.

Enter Winifrid *and the picture.*

So, hang it up.
I was enjoined by the party ought that picture,
Forty years since, ever when I was vex'd
To look upon that: what was his meaning in't,
I know not, but methinks upon the sudden
It has furnish'd me with mischief, such a plot
As never mother dreamt of. Here begins
My part i'th' play: my son's estate is sunk
By loss at sea, and he has nothing left
But the land his father left him. 'Tis concluded,
The law shall undo him. Come hither,
I have a weighty secret to impart;
But I would have thee first confirm to me
How I may trust that thou canst keep my counsel
Beyond death.

WINIFRID.
Why, mistress, 'tis your only way,
To enjoin me first that I reveal to you
The worst act I e'er did in all my life:
So one secret shall bind another.

368–369. Fetch . . . remember] *Dyce; one line in Q.*
369. S.D.] *Dyce; at l. 370 in Q.*
392. bind another] *Hazlitt;* bind one another *Q.*

369. *inner closet*] a small, very private room.
371. *salve*] remedy.
375. *ought*] that owned.
376. *since*] ago.

LEONORA.

Thou instruct'st me
Most ingenuously; for indeed it is not fit,
Where any act is plotted that is naught,
Any of counsel to it should be good;
And in a thousand ills have hapt i'th' world,
The intelligence of one another's shame
Have wrought far more effectually than the tie
Of conscience, or religion.

WINIFRID.

But think not, mistress,
That any sin which ever I committed
Did concern you; for proving false in one thing,
You were a fool if ever you would trust me
In the least matter of weight.

LEONORA.

Thou hast lived with me
These forty years; we have grown old together,
As many ladies and their women do,
With talking nothing, and with doing less.
We have spent our life in that which least concerns life,
Only in putting on our clothes; and now I think on't,
I have been a very courtly mistress to thee:
I have given thee good words, but no deeds. Now's the time
To requite all; my son has six lordships left him.

WINIFRID.

'Tis truth.

LEONORA.

But he cannot live four days to enjoy them.

WINIFRID.

Have you poisoned him?

LEONORA.

No. The poison is yet but brewing.

WINIFRID.

You must minister it to him with all privacy.

393. instruct'st] *Dyce;* instru'st *Q.*

---

394. *ingenuously*] ingeniously (cf. I.i.215 n.).
395. *naught*] wicked.

LEONORA.

Privacy? It shall be given him
In open court; I'll make him swallow it
Before the judge's face. If he be master
Of poor ten arpines of land forty hours longer,
Let the world repute me an honest woman.

WINIFRID.

So 'twill, I hope.

LEONORA. O, thou canst not conceive
My unimitable plot! Let's to my ghostly father,
Where first I will have thee make a promise
To keep my counsel; and then I will employ thee
In such a subtle combination,
Which will require, to make the practice fit,
Four devils, five advocates, to one woman's wit. *Exeunt.*

Explicit Actus Tertius.

[IV.i]

Enter Leonora, Sanitonella *at one door,* Winifrid, *Register; at the other,* Ariosto.

SANITONELLA [*to Register*].

Take her into your office, sir. She has that
In her belly, will dry up your ink, I can tell you.—
[*Exit Register with* Winifrid.]
[*To* Leonora.] This is the man that is your learned counsel,
A fellow that will trowl it off with tongue:
He never goes without restorative powder

431. one] *Q*(*corr.*); a *Q*(*uncorr.*).
[IV.i]
1. S.D.] *Lucas.*
1–2. *Dyce;* Take . . . in her/ Belly . . . you *Q*.
2.1.] *Lucas.*
3. S.D.] *Lucas.*

423. *arpines*] The arpent was a French land measure equaling a hundred square perches, roughly an acre.
426. *ghostly*] spiritual.
[IV.i]
4. *trowl it off*] speak facilely. To *trowl* the tongue was to move it nimbly (*OED*).

Of the lungs of fox in's pocket, and Malligo raisins
To make him long-winded. Sir, this gentlewoman
Entreats your counsel in an honest cause
Which, please you, sir, this brief, my own poor labor,
Will give you light of. [*Gives brief.*]

ARIOSTO.
Do you call this a brief?
Here's, as I weigh them, some fourscore sheets of paper.
What would they weigh if there were cheese wrapped in them,
Or figdates?

SANITONELLA. Joy come to you, you are merry;
We call this but a brief in our office.
The scope of the business lies i'th' margent.

ARIOSTO.
Methinks you prate too much.
I never could endure an honest cause
With a long prologue to't.

LEONORA. You trouble him.

ARIOSTO.
What's here? O strange! I have lived this sixty years,
Yet in all my practice never did shake hands
With a cause so odious. Sirrah, are you her knave?

SANITONELLA.
No, sir, I am a clerk.

10. S.D.] *Lucas.*
13–14.] *this edn.;* What . . . cheese/ Wrapt . . . Figdates./ Ioy . . . merry *Q.*
16. margent] *Q(corr.)*; Margent sheet *Q(uncorr.)*.

---

6. *lungs of fox*] believed beneficial to human lungs if one merely carried them with him.

6. *Malligo raisins*] made from Malaga grapes, which are named for the seaport in southern Spain. Gerard considered raisins effective in treating any problems of the lungs and voice.

11. *brief*] There is word play on shortness and on the legal brief, which ought to be "a summary of facts and points of law" pertaining to a case (*OED*).

14. *figdates*] small figs (Lucas), or perhaps small dates ("fig" could mean something small.

16. *scope*] main points.

16. *margent*] margin.

22. *knave*] servant.

ARIOSTO.

Why, you whoreson fogging rascal.
Are there not whores enow for presentations,
Of overseers, wrong the will o'th' dead,
Oppressions of widows or young orphans,
Wicked divorces, or your vicious cause
Of *Plus quam satis*, to content a woman,
But you must find new stratagems, new pursenets?
O, women, as the ballet lives to tell you,
What will you shortly come to!

SANITONELLA.

Your fee is ready, sir.

ARIOSTO.

The devil take such fees,
And all such suits i'th' tail of them! —See, the slave
Has writ false Latin! —Sirrah Ignoramus,
Were you ever at the university?

SANITONELLA.

Never, sir:
But 'tis well known to divers I have commenc'd
In a pew of our office.

ARIOSTO. Where? In a pew of your office!

SANITONELLA.

I have been dry-founder'd in't this four years,
Seldom found non-resident from my desk.

28. divorces] *Q(corr.)*; Diverses *Q(uncorr.)*.
30. pursenets] *Q(corr.)*; pursuits *Q(uncorr.)*.
36. Ignoramus] *Q(corr.)*; Ignorance *Q(uncorr.)*.
39. But'tis] *Q(corr.)*; It is *Q(uncorr.)*.
41. in't] *Q(corr.)*; with't *Q(uncorr.)*.

---

24. *fogging*] pettifogging, practicing legal chicanery.

25. *presentations*] presentments, the laying of formal statements before a court.

26. *overseers, wrong*] executors who wrong.

29. *Plus quam satis*] "more than enough," perhaps a charge of incontinency or adultery. Lucas connects it with *nunquam satis*, which seems to mean "impotence" when used out of legal context.

30. *pursenets*] bag-shaped nets whose mouths can be drawn shut; hence, any trap.

31. *ballet*] ballad; perhaps a reference to some popular broadside.

39. *commenc'd*] (1) taken a degree, as at a university; (2) begun.

40. *pew*] desk.

41. *dry-founder'd*] stuck fast.

ARIOSTO.

Non-resident subsumner!
I'll tear your libel for abusing that word,
By virtue of the clergy. [*Tears the brief.*]

SANITONELLA.

What do you mean, sir?
It cost me four nights' labor.

ARIOSTO.

Hadst thou been drunk so long,
Th'hadst done our court better service.

LEONORA.

Sir, you do forget your gravity, methinks.

ARIOSTO.

Cry ye mercy, do I so?
And as I take it, you do very little remember
Either womanhood, or Christianity. Why do ye meddle
With that seducing knave, that's good for nought,
Unless 't be to fill the office full of fleas
Or a winter itch, wears that spacious inkhorn
All a vacation only to cure tetters,
And his penknife to weed corns from the splay toes
Of the right worshipful of the office?

LEONORA.

You make bold with me, sir.

ARIOSTO.

Woman, y'are mad, I'll swear't, and have more need
Of a physician than a lawyer.
The melancholy humor flows in your face;
Your painting cannot hide it. Such vild suits

45. S.D.] *Dyce.*
49. Th'hadst] *this edn.;* T'hadst *Q.*

---

43. *subsumner*] not even a full-fledged summoner.

44. *libel*] plaintiff's written statement that starts a case.

44–45. *abusing . . . clergy*] literally, because the word "non-resident" ought to apply only to clergy wrongly living away from their charges; but also with a satiric twist on "virtue."

56. *winter itch*] skin eruption occurring in winter.

57. *tetters*] any skin eruption, such as eczema or ringworm. The tannin in ink supposedly cured it.

63. *melancholy . . . face*] The humor black bile supposedly caused melancholy, and seventeenth-century physiognomy would recognize its presence.

Disgrace our courts, and these make honest lawyers
Stop their own ears whilst they plead; and that's the reason
Your younger men that have good conscience
Wear such large nightcaps. Go, old woman, go pray,
For lunacy, or else the devil himself
Has ta'en possession of thee. May like cause
In any Christian court never find name!
Bad suits, and not the law, breed the law's shame. *Exit.*

LEONORA.
Sure the old man's frantic.

SANITONELLA.
Plague on's gouty fingers!
Were all of his mind, to entertain no suits
But such they thought were honest, sure our lawyers
Would not purchase half so fast.

Enter Contilupo, *a spruce lawyer.*

But here's the man,
Learned Signior Contilupo; here's a fellow
Of another piece, believe't. I must make shift
With the foul copy.

CONTILUPO. Business to me?

SANITONELLA.
To you, sir, from this lady.

CONTILUPO. She is welcome.

SANITONELLA.
'Tis a foul copy, sir; you'll hardly read it.
There's twenty double ducats; can you read, sir?

CONTILUPO.
Exceeding well, very, very exceeding well.

SANITONELLA [*aside*].
This man will be saved, he can read. Lord, lord,

72. breed] *this edn.;* bred (*past tense or alternative spelling of present?*) *Q*(*corr.*); breds *Q*(*uncorr.*).
77.1.] *Dyce; at l. 78 in Q.*
86. S.D.] *Dyce.*

68. *nightcaps*] the white caps or coifs worn by lawyers.
77. *purchase*] gain property.
80. *piece*] type.
81. *foul copy*] the rought draft; the fair copy has just been torn up.
86. *saved . . . read*] A criminal condemned to death might save himself by demonstrating that he could read ("benefit of clergy").

To see what money can do; be the hand never so foul,
Somewhat will be pick'd out on't.

CONTILUPO.
Is not this *vivere honeste*?

SANITONELLA.
No, that's struck out, sir;
And wherever you find *vivere honeste* in these papers,
Give it a dash, sir.

CONTILUPO. I shall be mindful of it.
In troth, you write a pretty secretary:
Your secretary hand ever takes best,
In mine opinion.

SANITONELLA. Sir, I have been in France
And there, believe't, your court hand generally
Takes beyond thought.

CONTILUPO.
Even as a man is traded in't.

SANITONELLA [*aside*].
That I could not think of this virtuous gentleman
Before I went to th' tother hog-rubber!
Why, this was wont to give young clerks half fees
To help him to clients. —Your opinion in the case, sir?

CONTILUPO.
I am struck with wonder, almost ecstasied,
With this most goodly suit.

LEONORA.
It is the fruit of a most hearty penitence.

CONTILUPO.
'Tis a case shall leave a precedent to all the world
In our succeeding annals, and deserves
Rather a spacious public theater

94–95. Your . . . opinion] *Dyce; one line in Q.*

99. S.D.] *Dyce.*

---

89. *vivere honeste*] "to live honest"; no claim is being made of honorable behavior.

93. *secretary*] handwriting style used in legal documents from the fifteenth to the seventeenth century.

96. *court hand*] handwriting used in English law-courts from the sixteenth into the early eighteenth century.

98. *traded*] experienced.

100. *hog-rubber*] a rustic, any low fellow.

Than a pent court for audence; it shall teach
All ladies the right path to rectify their issue.

SANITONELLA.
Lo you, here's a man of comfort.

CONTILUPO.
And you shall go unto a peaceful grave,
Discharg'd of such a guilt as would have lain
Howling forever at your wounded heart,
And rose with you to judgment.

SANITONELLA.
O give me such a lawyer, as will think
Of the day of judgment!

LEONORA.
You must urge the business against him
As spitefully as may be.

CONTILUPO.
Doubt not. What, is he summon'd?

SANITONELLA.
Yes, and the court will sit within this half hour.
Peruse your notes; you have very short warning.

CONTILUPO.
Never fear you that.
Follow me, worthy lady, and make account
This suit is ended already. *Exeunt.*

[IV.ii]

Enter Officers *preparing seats for the judges; to them* Ercole *muffled.*

FIRST OFFICER.
You would have a private seat, sir?

ERCOLE.
Yes, sir.

SECOND OFFICER.
Here's a closet belongs to th' court
Where you may hear all unseen.

116–117.] *Dyce; one line in Q.*

---

109. *pent*] confined.
109. *audence*] audience, hearing.
124. *make account*] consider that.

ERCOLE.

I thank you; there's money.

SECOND OFFICER.

I give you your thanks again, sir. [Ercole *withdraws*.]

Enter Contarino [*disguised as a Dane*], *the* Surgeons *disguised.*

CONTARINO.

Is't possible Romelio's persuaded
You are gone to the East Indies?

FIRST SURGEON.

Most confidently.

CONTARINO.

But do you mean to go?

SECOND SURGEON.

How? Go to the East Indies? And so many Hollanders gone to fetch sauce for their pickled herrings! Some have been pepper'd there too lately. But, I pray, being thus well recover'd of your wounds, why do you not reveal yourself?

CONTARINO.

That my fair Jolenta should be rumor'd
To be with child by noble Ercole,
Makes me expect to what a violent issue
These passages will come. I hear her brother
Is marrying the infant she goes with,
'Fore it be born; as, if it be a daughter,
To the Duke of Austria's nephew; if a son,
Into the noble ancient family
Of the Palavafini. He's a subtle devil;
And I do wonder what strange suit in law
Has hapt between him and's mother.

6. S.D.] *this edn.*
6.1.] *Dyce; at ll. 4–5 in Q; "disguised as a Dane" Lucas*
11. *How . . . Indies?*] *Dyce; one line in Q.*
14. *why . . . yourself*] *Dyce; one line in Q.*
19–20.] *Dyce;* Is . . . borne,/ As . . . Daughter *Q.*

11–13. *Hollanders . . . lately*] The Dutch, loading spices in the East Indies, had attacked four English ships picking up pepper in Sumatra in 1619 (Stoll), but some lesser skirmishes may be referred to.

17. *expect*] wait to see.

23. *Palavafini*] ? Pallavicini (Dyce).

FIRST SURGEON.
'Tis whisper'd 'mong the lawyers,
'Twill undo him forever.

Enter Sanitonella, Winifrid.

SANITONELLA.
Do you hear, officers?
You must take special care that you let in
No brachygraphy men to take notes.

FIRST OFFICER.
No, sir?

SANITONELLA.
By no means;
We cannot have a cause of any fame,
But you must have scurvy pamphlets and lewd ballets
Engender'd of it presently.
Have you broke fast yet?

WINIFRID.
Not I, sir.

SANITONELLA. 'Twas very ill done of you,
For this cause will be long a-pleading; but no matter,
I have a modicum in my buckram bag
To stop your stomach.

WINIFRID.
What is't? Green ginger?

SANITONELLA.
Green ginger, nor pellitory of Spain neither,
Yet 'twill stop a hollow tooth better than either of them.

WINIFRID.
Pray what is't?

SANITONELLA.
Look you,
It is a very lovely pudding-pie,
Which we clerks find great relief in.

---

30. *brachygraphy*] shorthand or stenography.

34. *ballets*] ballads.

41. *Green ginger*] undried ginger root.

42. *pellitory of Spain*] plant from Barbary whose pungent root can start saliva and ease toothache (*OED*).

46. *pudding-pie*] pie crust filled with a meat pudding, a sausage-like mixture.

WINIFRID.
I shall have no stomach.

SANITONELLA.
No matter; and you have not, I may pleasure
Some of our learned counsel with't; I have done it
Many a time and often, when a cause
Has proved like an after-game at Irish.

Enter Crispiano *like a judge, with another judge;* Contilupo *and another lawyer at one bar;* Romelio, Ariosto, *at another;* Leonora *with a black veil over her, and* Julio.

CRISPIANO.
'Tis a strange suit. Is Leonora come?

CONTILUPO.
She's here, my lord. Make way there for the lady.

CRISPIANO.
Take off her veil; it seems she is ashamed
To look her cause i'th' face.

CONTILUPO. She's sick, my lord.

ARIOSTO.
She's mad, my lord, and would be kept more dark.—
[*To* Romelio.] By your favor, sir, I have now occasion
To be at your elbow, and within this half hour
Shall entreat you to be angry, very angry.

CRISPIANO.
Is Romelio come?

ROMELIO.
I am here, my lord, and call'd, I do protest,
To answer what I know not, for as yet
I am wholly ignorant of what the court
Will charge me with.

CRISPIANO. I assure you, the proceeding
Is most unequal then, for I perceive

58. S.D.] *Dyce.*
58–60.] *Dyce;* prose in *Q.*

52. *after-game*] the second game, generally played painstakingly in an attempt to even up the score.

52. *Irish*] an old form of backgammon.

57. *mad . . . dark*] Solitary confinement in a dark place was a common treatment for a mad person.

The counsel of the adverse party furnish'd
With full instruction.

ROMELIO.
Pray, my lord, who is my accuser?

CRISPIANO.
'Tis your mother.

ROMELIO [*aside*].
She has discovered Contarino's murder—
If she prove so unnatural, to call
My life in question, I am arm'd to suffer
This to end all my losses.

CRISPIANO.
Sir, we will do you this favor:
You shall hear the accusation,
Which being known, we will adjourn the court
Till a fortnight hence: you may provide your counsel.

ARIOSTO.
I advise you, take their proffer,
Or else the lunacy runs in a blood,
You are more mad than she.

ROMELIO. What are you, sir?

ARIOSTO.
An angry fellow that would do thee good,
For goodness' sake itself, I do protest,
Neither for love nor money.

ROMELIO.
Prithee stand further; I shall gall your gout else.

ARIOSTO.
Come, come, I know you for an East Indy merchant;
You have a spice of pride in you still.

ROMELIO.
My lord, I am so strengthen'd in my innocence
For any the least shadow of a crime

71. S.D.] *Dyce.*

---

80. *a*] the.

85. *gall . . . gout*] make it uncomfortable by physical contact, presumably by stepping on gouty toes.

87. *spice*] trace (appropriate for a merchant trading with the Spice Islands, as the East Indies were called).

89. *For*] of.

Committed 'gainst my mother or the world
That she can charge me with, here do I make it
My humble suit, only this hour and place
May give it as full hearing, and as free
And unrestrain'd a sentence.

CRISPIANO.
Be not too confident; you have cause to fear.

ROMELIO.
Let fear dwell with earthquakes,
Shipwracks at sea, or prodigies in heaven:
I cannot set myself so many fathom
Beneath the height of my true heart as fear.

ARIOSTO.
Very fine words, I assure you, if they were
To any purpose.

CRISPIANO. Well, have your entreaty;
And if your own credulity undo you,
Blame not the court hereafter. Fall to your plea.

CONTILUPO.
May it please your lordship and the reverend court
To give me leave to open to you a case
So rare, so altogether void of precedent,
That I do challenge all the spacious volumes
Of the whole civil law to show the like.
We are of counsel for this gentlewoman;
We have receiv'd our fee, yet the whole course
Of what we are to speak is quite against her;
Yet we'll deserve our fee, too. There stands one,
Romelio the merchant. I will name him to you
Without either title or addition,
For those false beams of his supposed honor,
As void of true heat as are all painted fires
Or glowworms in the dark, suit him all basely,
As if he had bought his gentry from the herald

95. confident;] *no visible punctuation mark in some copies of Q inverts the meaning.*

100–101. Very . . . purpose] *Dyce; one line in Q.*

---

99. *as fear*] as to fear.

114. *addition*] distinguishing form of address.

117. *suit*] with a second meaning of clothing a person, perhaps in anticipation of ll. 120–122.

With money got by extortion: I will first
Produce this Aesop's crow, as he stands forfeit
For the long use of his gay borrowed plumes,
And then let him hop naked. I come to th' point:
T'as been a dream in Naples, very near
This eight and thirty years, that this Romelio
Was nobly descended; he has rank'd himself
With the nobility, shamefully usurp'd
Their place, and in a kind of saucy pride,
Which, like to mushrooms, ever grow most rank
When they do spring from dunghills, sought to o'ersway
The Fliski, the Grimaldi, Dori,
And all the ancient pillars of our state;
View now what he is come to, this poor thing
Without a name, this cuckoo hatch'd i'th' nest
Of a hedge sparrow!

ROMELIO. Speaks he all this to me?

ARIOSTO.
Only to you, sir.

ROMELIO.
I do not ask thee; prithee hold thy prating.

ARIOSTO.
Why, very good, you will be presently
As angry as I could wish.

CONTILUPO.
What title shall I set to this base coin?
He has no name, and for's aspect, he seems
A giant in a May-game, that within
Is nothing but a porter. I'll undertake,
He had as good have travel'd all his life
With gypsies: I will sell him to any man
For an hundred chickeens, and he that buys him of me
Shall lose by th' hand, too.

---

120. *Aesop's crow*] the daw that clothed himself in peacock's feathers.

130. *Fliski*] Fieschi (Dyce).

130. *Grimaldi, Dori*] With the Fieschi, the Doria and Grimaldi families were three of the most important in Genoa.

141–142. *giant . . . porter*] with reference to the men who carried wooden frameworks supporting giant figures at May Day festivities.

144. *gypsies*] any wandering rogues.

145. *chickeens*] zecchins, gold coins originating in Venice and generally worth about $2.50.

ARIOSTO.
Lo, what you are come to,
You that did scorn to trade in anything
But gold or spices, or your cochineal!
He rates you now at poor John.

ROMELIO.
Out upon thee! I would thou wert of his side.

ARIOSTO.
Would you so?

ROMELIO.
The devil and thee together on each hand,
To prompt the lawyer's memory when he founders.

CRISPIANO.
Signior Contilupo, the court holds it fit
You leave this stale declaiming 'gainst the person,
And come to the matter.

CONTILUPO. Now I shall, my lord.

CRISPIANO.
It shows a poor malicious eloquence,
And it is strange, men of your gravity
Will not forgo it: verily, I presume,
If you but heard yourself speaking with my ears,
Your phrase would be more modest.

CONTILUPO.
Good my lord, be assured,
I will leave all circumstance, and come to th' purpose:
This Romelio is a bastard.

ROMELIO.
How, a bastard? O, mother,
Now the day begins grow hot on your side!

CONTILUPO.
Why, she is your accuser.

ROMELIO.
I had forgot that; was my father married

169–171. I . . . begetting] *Dyce; prose in Q.*

---

149. *cochineal*] scarlet dye made from dried insects.
150. *rates . . . John*] considers you of the value of dried hake, a very cheap fish.

To any other woman at the time
Of my begetting?

CONTILUPO. That's not the business.

ROMELIO.

I turn me, then, to you that were my mother,
But by what name I am to call you now,
You must instruct me: were you ever married
To my father?

LEONORA.

To my shame I speak it, never.

CRISPIANO.

Not to Francisco Romelio?

LEONORA.

May it please your lordships,
To him I was, but he was not his father.

CONTILUPO.

Good my lord, give us leave in a few words
To expound the riddle, and to make it plain
Without the least of scruple; for I take it,
There cannot be more lawful proof i'th' world
Than the oath of the mother.

CRISPIANO.

Well then, to your proofs, and be not tedious.

CONTILUPO.

I'll conclude in a word.
Some nine and thirty years since, which was the time
This woman was married, Francisco Romelio,
This gentleman's putative father and her husband,
Being not married to her past a fortnight,
Would needs go travel; did so, and continued
In France and the Low Countries eleven months.
Take special note o'th' time, I beseech your lordship,
For it makes much to th' business. In his absence,
He left behind to sojourn at his house
A Spanish gentleman, a fine spruce youth
By the lady's confession, and you may be sure
He was no eunuch neither; he was one
Romelio loved very dearly, as oft haps,

189. *putative*] reputed.

No man alive more welcome to the husband
Than he that makes him cuckold. This gentleman,
I say, breaking all laws of hospitality,
Got his friend's wife with child, a full two months
'Fore the husband returned.

SANITONELLA [*aside*].
Good sir, forget not the lambskin.

CONTILUPO [*aside*].
I warrant thee.

SANITONELLA [*aside*].
I will pinch by the buttock, to put you in mind of't.

CONTILUPO [*aside*].
Prithee hold thy prating.—
[*To* Crispiano.] What's to be practic'd now, my lord?
Marry, this:
Romelio being a young novice, not acquainted
With this precedence, very innocently
Returning home from travel, finds his wife
Grown an excellent good huswife, for she had set
Her women to spin flax, and to that use
Had, in a study which was built of stone,
Stor'd up at least an hundreth weight of flax:
Marry, such a thread as was to be spun from the flax,
I think the like was never heard of.

CRISPIANO.
What was that?

CONTILUPO.
You may be certain, she would lose no time
In bragging that her husband had got up

201–202.] *this edn.;* Then . . . Cuckold./ This . . . say,/ Breaking . . . Hospitalitie *Q*.
205. S.D.] *Lucas.*
206. S.D.] *Lucas.*
207. S.D.] *Lucas.*
208. S.D.] *Lucas.*
209. S.D.] *this edn.*

213. *huswife*] housewife, with a second meaning of "hussy," a loose woman.
215. *study*] a private room or office of the master of the house.
216. *hundreth weight*] 112 pounds.
217. *thread*] Contilupo picks up the figurative meaning—the thread of a story, a "yarn."

Her belly: to be short, at seven months' end,
Which was the time of her delivery,
And when she felt herself to fall in travail,
She makes her waiting-woman, as by mischance,
Set fire to the flax; the fright whereof,
As they pretend, causes this gentlewoman
To fall in pain, and be delivered
Eight weeks afore her reckoning.

SANITONELLA [*aside*].
Now, sir, remember the lambskin.

CONTILUPO.
The midwife straight howls out, there was no hope
Of th'infant's life; swaddles it in a flay'd lambskin,
As a bird hatch'd too early; makes it up
With three quarters of a face, that made it look
Like a changeling; cries out to Romelio
To have it christen'd, lest it should depart
Without that it came for: and thus are many serv'd
That take care to get gossips for those children
To which they might be godfathers themselves,
And yet be no arch-Puritans neither.

CRISPIANO. No more!

ARIOSTO.
Pray, my lord, give him way: you spoil his oratory else.
Thus would they jest, were they fee'd to open
Their sister's cases.

CRISPIANO. You have urged enough;
You first affirm, her husband was away from her
Eleven months?

CONTILUPO.
Yes, my lord.

222. months'] *Dyce;* moneths *Q*.
226. fright] *Dyce;* flight *Q*.
230. S.D.] *Lucas*.
241–243. Pray . . . cases] *Dyce; prose in Q*.

235. *changeling*] a child, often malformed, believed left by fairies in exchange for the proper baby.

238–239. *gossips . . . godfathers*] Anglican church-law forbade a person to be a godparent (*gossip*) of his own child.

240. *arch-Puritans*] Puritans felt that the parents ought to be the god-parents (Lucas).

CRISPIANO.

And at seven months' end
After his return, she was delivered
Of this Romelio, and had gone her full time?

CONTILUPO.

True, my lord.

CRISPIANO.

So by this account this gentleman was begot
In his supposed father's absence?

CONTILUPO.

You have it fully.

CRISPIANO.

A most strange suit this: 'tis beyond example,
Either time past or present, for a woman
To publish her own dishonor voluntarily,
Without being called in question, some forty years
After the sin committed, and her counsel
To enlarge the offense with as much oratory,
As ever I did hear them in my life
Defend a guilty woman; 'tis most strange:
Or why with such a poisoned violence
Should she labor her son's undoing? We observe
Obedience of creatures to the law of Nature
Is the stay of the whole world; here that law is broke,
For though our civil law makes difference
'Tween the base and the legitimate,
Compassionate Nature makes them equal, nay,
She many times prefers them. I pray resolve me,
Sir, have not you and your mother
Had some suit in law together lately?

ROMELIO.

None, my lord.

CRISPIANO.

No? No contention about parting your goods?

ROMELIO.

Not any.

247. months'] *Dyce;* moneths *Q.*

267–270.] *this edn.;* Tween . . . Nature/ Makes . . . prefers them./I . . . mother *Q.*

CRISPIANO.
No flaw, no unkindness?

ROMELIO.
None that ever arrived at my knowledge.

CRISPIANO.
Bethink yourself, this cannot choose but savor
Of a woman's malice deeply; and I fear
Y'are practic'd upon most devilishly.
How happ'd, gentlewoman, you reveal'd this no sooner?

LEONORA.
While my husband lived, my lord, I durst not.

CRISPIANO.
I should rather ask you why you reveal it now.

LEONORA.
Because, my lord, I loath'd that such a sin
Should lie smother'd with me in my grave; my penitence,
Though to my shame, prefers the revealing of it
'Bove worldly reputation.

CRISPIANO. Your penitence!
Might not your penitence have been as hearty,
Though it had never summon'd to the court
Such a conflux of people?

LEONORA.
Indeed, I might have confess'd it privately
To th' church, I grant; but you know repentance
Is nothing without satisfaction.

CRISPIANO.
Satisfaction? Why, your husband's dead;
What satisfaction can you make him?

LEONORA.
The greatest satisfaction in the world, my lord:
To restore the land to th' right heir, and that's
My daughter.

CRISPIANO.
O, she's straight begot, then?

290–291.] *Dyce;* Indeed . . . it,/ Priuately . . . repentance *Q.*

296–297.] *Dyce; one line in Q.*

287. *hearty*] heartfelt.

ARIOSTO.

Very well: may it please this honorable court,
If he be a bastard, and must forfeit his land for't,
She has proved herself a strumpet, and must lose
Her dower. Let them go a-begging together.

SANITONELLA.

Who shall pay us our fees, then?

CRISPIANO.

Most just.

ARIOSTO.

You may see now what an old house
You are like to pull over your head, dame.

ROMELIO.

Could I conceive this publication
Grew from a hearty penitence, I could bear
My undoing the more patiently; but, my lord,
There is no reason, as you said even now,
To satisfy me but this suit of hers
Springs from a devilish malice; and her pretense
Of a grieved conscience and religion,
Like to the horrid Powder-Treason in England,
Has a most bloody unnatural revenge
Hid under it. O, the violencies of women!
Why, they are creatures made up and compounded
Of all monsters, poisoned minerals,
And sorcerous herbs that grows.

ARIOSTO. Are you angry yet?

ROMELIO.

Would man express a bad one,
Let him forsake all natural example,

320. man] *Dyce;* men *Q*.

301–302. *She . . . dower*] By law, Leonora would not forfeit her dowry unless she had taken up residence with her lover (Lucas citing 13 Edward I, c. 34).

311. *but*] but that.

314. *Powder-Treason*] Catholic plot to blow up the Houses of Parliament on November 5, 1605, when King, Lords, and Commons were gathered for the opening.

315. *revenge*] probably the personal grudge of Thomas Percy against King James (Lucas).

320. *express a bad one*] say how bad a woman is.

And compare one to another; they have no more mercy
Than ruinous fires in great tempests.

ARIOSTO.
Take heed you do not crack your voice, sir.

ROMELIO.
Hard-hearted creatures, good for nothing else
But to wind dead bodies.

ARIOSTO.
Yes, to weave seaming lace with the bones
Of their husbands that were long since buried,
And curse them when they tangle.

ROMELIO.
Yet why do I
Take bastardy so distastefully, when i'th' world
A many things that are essential parts
Of greatness are but by-slips, and are father'd
On the wrong parties?
Preferment in the world a many times
Basely begotten? Nay, I have observ'd
The immaculate justice of a poor man's cause,
In such a court as this, has not known whom
To call father, which way to direct itself
For compassion—but I forget my temper!
Only, that I may stop that lawyer's throat,
I do beseech the court, and the whole world,
They will not think the baselier of me
For the vice of a mother; for that woman's sin,
To which you all dare swear when it was done,
I would not give my consent.

CRISPIANO.
Stay, here's an accusation,
But here's no proof. What was the Spaniard's name
You accuse of adultery?

327–329. Yes . . . tangle] *Hazlitt; prose in Q.*

---

327. *seaming lace*] narrow lace either inserted in or covering a seam.

327. *bones*] Bone bobbins were sometimes used in lace-making.

332. *by-slips*] bastards, with an overtone of the second meaning, trivial faults.

336. *immaculate*] pure (with ironic overtones).

345. *consent*] "agreement of opinion" (*OED*); he may be denying either the ease of dating, or the fact of adultery.

CONTILUPO.

Don Crispiano, my lord.

CRISPIANO.

What part of Spain was he born in?

CONTILUPO.

In Castile.

JULIO [*aside*].

This may prove my father.

SANITONELLA [*aside*].

And my master: my client's spoil'd, then.

CRISPIANO.

I knew that Spaniard well: if you be a bastard,
Such a man being your father, I dare vouch you
A gentleman; and in that, Signior Contilupo,
Your oratory went a little too far.
When do we name Don John of Austria,
The Emperor's son, but with reverence?
And I have known, in divers families,
The bastards the greater spirits. But to th' purpose:
What time was this gentleman begot?
And be sure you lay your time right.

ARIOSTO.

Now the metal comes to the touchstone.

CONTILUPO.

In anno seventy-one, my lord.

CRISPIANO.

Very well, seventy-one: the Battle
Of Lepanto was fought in't; a most remarkable time,
'Twill lie for no man's pleasure; and what proof is there,
More than the affirmation of the mother,
Of this corporal dealing?

352. S.D.] *Lucas.*
353. S.D.] *Lucas.*
366–370.] *this edn.;* Very . . . one:/ The . . . in't,/ A . . . pleasure:/ And . . . the/ Mother . . . dealing? *Q.*

358. *Don John of Austria*] illegitimate but officially acknowledged son of Charles V.

366–367. *Battle/ Of Lepanto*] on October 7; a naval victory over the Turks by Spanish, Venetian, and Papal forces under Don John.

CONTILUPO.
The deposition of a waiting-woman
Served her the same time.

CRISPIANO. Where is she?

CONTILUPO.
Where is our solicitor with the waiting-woman?

ARIOSTO.
Room for the bag and baggage.

SANITONELLA.
Here, my lord, *ore tenus*.

CRISPIANO.
And what can you say, gentlewoman?

WINIFRID.
Please your lordship, I was the party that dealt
In the business, and brought them together.

CRISPIANO.
Well.

WINIFRID.
And conveyed letters between them.

CRISPIANO.
What needed letters, when 'tis said he lodg'd in her house?

WINIFRID.
A running ballad now and then to her viol,
For he was never well but when he was fiddling.

CRISPIANO.
Speak to the purpose: did you ever
Know them bed together?

WINIFRID. No, my lord,
But I have brought him to the bed side.

CRISPIANO.
That was somewhat near to the business.
And what, did you help him off with his shoes?

WINIFRID.
He wore no shoes, an't please you, my lord.

371–372. The . . . time] *this edn.; prose in Q.*

384–385. Speak . . . together] *Hazlitt; prose in Q.*

375. *ore tenus*] "by word of mouth," probably meaning "ready to testify in person."

382. *running*] smooth and rapid.

CRISPIANO.
No? What then, pumps?

WINIFRID.
Neither.

CRISPIANO.
Boots were not fit for his journey.

WINIFRID.
He wore tennis-court woolen slippers,
For fear of creaking, sir, and making a noise,
To wake the rest o'th' house.

CRISPIANO.
Well, and what did he there,
In his tennis-court woolen slippers?

WINIFRID.
Please your lordship, question me in Latin.
For the cause is very foul; the examiner o'th' court
Was fain to get it out of me alone i'th' countinghouse,
'Cause he would not spoil the youth o'th' office.

ARIOSTO.
Here's a Latin spoon, and a long one,
To feed with the devil!

WINIFRID.
I'd be loath to be ignorant that way,
For I hope to marry a proctor, and take my pleasure abroad
At the commencements with him.

ARIOSTO.
Come closer to the business.

WINIFRID.
I will come as close as modesty will give me leave.
Truth is, every morning when he lay with her,

---

390. *pumps*] lightweight shoes, generally for indoor wear.
393. *tennis-court woolen slippers*] Felt-soled slippers were worn for playing tennis on indoor courts.
402–403. *Latin . . . devil*] There is a pun on latten (brass), and a reference to the old proverb on using a long spoon when supping with the devil.
405. *proctor*] a kind of attorney in civil or ecclesiastical courts.
405. *abroad*] anywhere out of her own house.
406. *commencements*] beginning of law terms.

I made a caudle for him, by the appointment
Of my mistress, which he would still refuse,
And call for small drink.

CRISPIANO. Small drink?

ARIOSTO. For a julep.

WINIFRID.
And said he was wondrous thirsty.

CRISPIANO.
What's this to the purpose?

WINIFRID. Most effectual, my lord.
I have heard them laugh together extremely, and the curtain rods fall from the tester of the bed; and he ne'er came from her, but he thrust money in my hand; and once, in truth, he would have had some dealing with me; which, I took, he thought 'twould be the only way i'th' world to make me keep counsel the better.

SANITONELLA [*aside*].
That's a stinger; 'tis a good wench, be not daunted.

CRISPIANO.
Did you ever find the print of two in the bed?

WINIFRID.
What a question's that to be ask'd! May it please your lordship, 'tis to be thought he lay nearer to her than so.

CRISPIANO.
What age are you of, gentlewoman?

WINIFRID.
About six-and-forty, my lord.

CRISPIANO.
Anno seventy-one,
And Romelio is thirty-eight: by that reckoning,

415–416. I . . . bed] *this edn.;* I . . . extreamely,/ And . . . bed *Q* (*remainder of speech in prose in Q*).
418–419. me . . . he] *this edn.;* mee, which I tooke; he *Q*.
421. S.D.] *Lucas.*

410. *caudle*] a warm, thin gruel, spiced or sweetened and fortified with ale or wine, generally given to strengthen a person.
412. *small drink*] weak, perhaps non-alcoholic drink.
412. *julep*] a sweet drink; figuratively, "something to cool the heat of passion" (*OED*).
416. *tester*] the fittings and frame that held the bed curtains and canopy.
419. *took*] assumed.
421. *stinger*] sharp argument.

You were a bawd at eight year old. Now, verily,
You fell to the trade betimes.

SANITONELLA [*aside*].
There y'are from the bias.

WINIFRID.
I do not know my age directly; sure I am elder.
I can remember two great frosts, and three great plagues,
And the loss of Callis, and the first coming up
Of the breeches with the great codpiece;
And I pray what age do you take me of, then?

SANITONELLA [*aside*].
Well come off again.

ARIOSTO.
An old hunted hare: she has all her doubles.

ROMELIO.
For your own gravities,
And the reverence of the court, I do beseech you,
Rip up the cause no further, but proceed to sentence.

CRISPIANO.
One question more, and I have done:
Might not this Crispiano, this Spaniard,
Lie with your mistress at some other time,
Either afore or after, than i'th' absence
Of her husband?

LEONORA.
Never.

CRISPIANO.
Are you certain of that?

LEONORA. On my soul, never.

431. S.D.] *Lucas.*
437. S.D.] *Lucas.*
445–446.] *Dyce; one line in Q.*

430. *betimes*] early.
431. *from the bias*] off the set course.
433. *two great frosts*] probably 1564 and 1607.
433. *three great plagues*] probably 1563, 1592–1594, and 1603.
434. *Callis*] Calais, lost by the English in 1558 after two centuries' occupation.
434–435. *first . . . codpiece*] men's fashion event relatively early (c. 1520) in Henry VIII's reign.
438. *doubles*] tricks, deceits.

CRISPIANO.
That's well—he never lay with her,
But in anno seventy-one; let that be remember'd.—
Stand you aside a while. Mistress, the truth is,
I knew this Crispiano, lived in Naples
At the same time, and loved the gentleman
As my bosom friend; and, as I do remember,
The gentleman did leave his picture with you,
If age or neglect have not in so long time
Ruin'd it.

LEONORA. I preserve it still, my lord.

CRISPIANO.
I pray let me see't, let me see the face
I then loved so much to look on.

LEONORA. Fetch it.

WINIFRID.
I shall, my lord.

CRISPIANO. No, no, gentlewoman,
I have other business for you.

[*Exit an officer for the picture.*]

FIRST SURGEON [*aside*].
Now were the time to cut Romelio's throat,
And accuse him for your murder.

CONTARINO [*aside*]. By no means.

SECOND SURGEON [*aside*].
Will you not let us be men of fashion,
And down with him now he's going?

CONTARINO [*aside*].
Peace! Let's attend the sequel.

CRISPIANO.
I commend you, lady;
There was a main matter of conscience.
How many ills spring from adultery!
First, the supreme law that is violated;
Nobility oft stain'd with bastardy;
Inheritance of land falsely possess'd;

456–457. If . . . Ruin'd it] *Dyce; one line in Q*.
461.1.] *this edn.*
462. S.D.] *Lucas.*
463. S.D.] *Lucas.*
464. S.D.] *Lucas.*
466. S.D.] *Lucas.*

The husband scorn'd, wife sham'd, and babes unblest.

The picture [*is brought in*].

So, hang it up i'th' court. You have heard
What has been urged 'gainst Romelio.
Now my definitive sentence in this cause
Is, I will give no sentence at all.

ARIOSTO. No?

CRISPIANO.

No, I cannot, for I am made a party.

SANITONELLA [*aside*].

How, a party? Here are fine cross tricks.
What the devil will he do now?

CRISPIANO.

Signior Ariosto, his Majesty of Spain
Confers my place upon you by this patent,
Which till this urgent hour I have kept
From your knowledge. May you thrive in't, noble sir,
And do that which but few in our place do,
Go to their grave uncurs'd!

ARIOSTO. This law-business
Will leave me so small leisure to serve God,
I shall serve the King the worse.

SANITONELLA [*aside*].

Is he a judge?
We must then look for all conscience and no law;
He'll beggar all his followers.

CRISPIANO [*to* Romelio].

Sir, I am of your counsel, for the cause in hand
Was begun at such a time, 'fore you could speak;
You had need therefore have one speak for you.

ARIOSTO.

Stay, I do here first make protestation,
I ne'er took fee of this Romelio

473.1.] *Dyce;* "*The picture*" *at l. 474 in Q.*
479. S.D.] *Lucas.*
489. S.D.] *Lucas.*
492. S.D.] *Lucas.*

479. *cross tricks*] things at variance with the main course of action, distractions.

482. *patent*] official document granting authority.

For being of his counsel; which may free me,
Being now his judge, fro' the imputation
Of taking a bribe. Now, sir, speak your mind.

CRISPIANO.
I do first entreat, that the eyes of all here present
May be fix'd upon this.

LEONORA [*aside*].
O, I am confounded! This is Crispiano.

JULIO [*aside*].
This is my father; how the judges have bleated him!

WINIFRID [*aside*].
You may see truth will out in spite of the devil.

CRISPIANO.
Behold, I am the shadow of this shadow;
Age has made me so. Take from me forty years,
And I was such a summer fruit as this,
At least the painter feigned so; for indeed,
Painting and epitaphs are both alike:
They flatter us, and say we have been thus.
But I am the party here that stands accused
For adultery with this woman, in the year
Seventy-one; now I call you, my lord, to witness,
Four years before that time I went to th'Indies,
And till this month, did never set my foot since
In Europe; and for any former incontinence,
She has vowed there was never any. What remains then,
But this is a mere practice 'gainst her son?
And I beseech the court it may be sifted
And most severely punish'd.

SANITONELLA [*aside*].
Ud's foot, we are spoiled;
Why, my client's proved an honest woman.

498. fro'] *Hazlitt;* for *Q*.
502. S.D.] *Lucas.*
503. S.D.] *Lucas.*
504. S.D.] *Lucas.*
521. S.D.] *Lucas.*

503. *bleated*] cried at; perhaps "bleated about" is closer to Webster's intention. Lucas suggests "bleared," with a sense of confusing.

519. *sifted*] examined closely to discover the truth.

522. *honest*] chaste.

WINIFRID [*aside*].
What do you think will become of me now?

SANITONELLA [*aside*].
You'll be made dance lacrymae, I fear, at a cart's tail.

ARIOSTO.
You, mistress, where are you now?
Your tennis-court slips and your ta'en drink
In a morning for your hot liver? Where's the man
Would have had some dealing with you, that you might
Keep counsel the better?

WINIFRID.
May it please the court, I am but a young thing,
And was drawn arsy varsy into the business.

ARIOSTO.
How young? Of five-and-forty?

WINIFRID.
Five-and-forty! And shall please you,
I am not five-and-twenty:
She made me color my hair with bean-flour,
To seem elder than I was; and then my rotten teeth,
With eating sweetmeats—why, should a farrier
Look in my mouth, he might mistake my age.
O mistress, mistress, you are an honest woman,
And you may be asham'd on't, to abuse the court thus.

LEONORA.
Whatsoe'er I have attempted
'Gainst my own fame, or the reputation
Of that gentleman my son, the Lord Contarino
Was cause of it.

CONTARINO [*aside*].
Who, I?

523. S.D.] *Lucas.*
524. S.D.] *Lucas.*
545. S.D.] *Dyce.*

---

524. *dance lacrymae*] i.e., whipped; offenders were tied to the backs of carts and whipped through the streets, sorrowing as they went.

527. *hot liver*] lust; the liver was believed to be the seat of love and violent passions.

531. *arsy varsy*] hindside foremost and, presumably, unwillingly.

540. *abuse*] deceive, as well as ill-use.

ARIOSTO.
He that should have married your daughter?
It was a plot, belike then, to confer
The land on her that should have been his wife.

LEONORA.
More than I have said already, all the world
Shall ne'er extract from me; I entreat from both
Your equal pardons.

JULIO. And I from you, sir.

CRISPIANO.
Sirrah, stand you aside;
I will talk with you hereafter.

JULIO.
I could never away with after-reckonings.

LEONORA.
And now, my lords, I do most voluntarily
Confine myself unto a stricter prison
And a severer penance than this court
Can impose: I am enter'd into religion.

CONTARINO [*aside*].
I the cause of this practice! —This ungodly woman
Has sold herself to falsehood: I will now reveal myself.

ERCOLE [*coming forward, addressing* Ariosto].
Stay, my lord, here's a window
To let in more light to the court.

CONTARINO [*aside*].
Mercy upon me! O, that thou art living
Is mercy indeed!

FIRST SURGEON [*aside*].
Stay, keep in your shell a little longer!

ERCOLE.
I am Ercole.

ARIOSTO.
A guard upon him for the death of Contarino!

557–558.] *Dyce;* And . . . impose,/ I . . . Religion *Q*.
559. S.D.] *Dyce.*
563. S.D.] *Dyce.*
565. S.D.] *Hazlitt.*

554. *away with*] put up with (*OED*).

ERCOLE.
I obey the arrest o'th' court.

ROMELIO.
O, sir, you are happily restored to life
And to us your friends!

ERCOLE. Away, thou art the traitor
I only live to challenge. This former suit
Touch'd but thy fame; this accusation
Reaches to thy fame and life. The brave Contarino
Is generally supposed slain by this hand—

CONTARINO [*aside*].
How knows he the contrary?

ERCOLE. But truth is,
Having received from me some certain wounds
Which were not mortal, this vild murderer,
Being by will deputed overseer
Of the nobleman's estate to his sister's use,
That he might make him sure from surviving
To revoke that will, stole to him in's bed and kill'd him.

ROMELIO.
Strange, unheard of, more practice yet!

ARIOSTO.
What proof of this?

ERCOLE.
The report of his mother delivered to me,
In distraction for Contarino's death.

CONTARINO [*aside*].
For my death? I begin to apprehend,
That the violence of this woman's love to me
Might practice the disinheriting of her son.

ARIOSTO.
What say you to this, Leonora?

LEONORA.
Such a thing I did utter out of my distraction:
But how the court will censure that report,
I leave to their wisdoms.

575. S.D.] *Dyce.*
580. sure from] *Q(corr.)*; sure *Q(uncorr.)*.
586. S.D.] *Dyce.*

580. *make . . . surviving*] make sure he will not survive.

ARIOSTO.
My opinion is,
That this late slander urged against her son
Takes from her all manner of credit:
She that would not stick to deprive him of his living,
Will as little tender his life.

LEONORA.
I beseech the court,
I may retire myself to my place of penance
I have vowed myself and my woman.

ARIOSTO.
Go when you please. [*Exeunt* Leonora *and* Winifrid.]
[*To* Ercole.] What should move you
Be thus forward in the accusation?

ERCOLE.
My love to Contarino.

ARIOSTO.
O, it bore very bitter fruit at your last meeting.

ERCOLE.
'Tis true; but I begun to love him
When I had most cause to hate him; when our bloods
Embrac'd each other, then I pitied
That so much valor should be hazarded
On the fortune of a single rapier,
And not spent against the Turk.

ARIOSTO.
Stay, sir, be well advised:
There is no testimony but your own
[*To* Romelio.] To approve you slew him, therefore no other way
To decide it, but by duel.

CONTARINO.
Yes, my lord, I dare affirm 'gainst all the world,
This nobleman speaks truth.

ARIOSTO.
You will make yourself a party in the duel.

600. S.D. *Exeunt . . .* Winifrid] *Dyce.*
600. S.D. *To* Ercole] *Lucas.*
612. S.D.] *suggested by Lucas.*
615. nobleman] *Dyce;* Noble man *Q.*

ROMELIO.

Let him; I will fight with them both, sixteen of them.

ERCOLE.

Sir, I do not know you.

CONTARINO.

Yes, but you have forgot me; you and I
Have sweat in the breach together at Malta.

ERCOLE.

Cry you mercy, I have known of your nation
Brave soldiers.

JULIO [*aside*].

Now, if my father
Have any true spirit in him, I'll recover
His good opinion. —[*To* Contarino.] Do you hear? Do not swear, sir,
For I dare swear that you will swear a lie,
A very filthy, stinking, rotten lie;
And if the lawyers think not this sufficient,
I'll give the lie in the stomach—
That's somewhat deeper than the throat—
Both here, and all France over and over,
From Marselys, or Bayon, to Callis sands,
And there draw my sword upon thee,
And new scour it in the gravel of thy kidneys.

ARIOSTO.

You the defendant charged with the murder,
And you second there,
Must be committed to the custody

619–620.] *Dyce;* Yes . . . sweat/ In . . . Malta *Q*.

623. S.D.] *Dyce.*

625. S.D.] *Lucas.*

---

620. *in . . . Malta*] The Knights of Malta repulsed a major attack by the Turks in 1565, although a lesser action may be in Webster's mind.

621. *Cry you mercy*] I ask your mercy or pardon.

621. *your nation*] Contarino is still disguised as a Dane.

629. *in the stomach*] A "lie in the throat" was worse than a mere lie, and this may be an attempt at an even more severe accusation, as well as a reference to proving him a liar by running him through the body.

632. *Marselys*] Marseilles.

632. *Bayon*] Bayonne, in southwestern France.

632. *Callis sands*] Calais was close to England and duels, illegal in England, could be fought there.

Of the Knight-Marshal; and the court gives charge
They be tomorrow ready in the lists
Before the sun be risen.

ROMELIO.
I do entreat the court there be a guard
Placed o'er my sister, that she enter not
Into religion: she's rich, my lords,
And the persuasions of friars, to gain
All her possessions to their monasteries,
May do much upon her.

ARIOSTO.
We'll take order for her.

CRISPIANO.
There's a nun too you have got with child:
How will you dispose of her?

ROMELIO.
You question me as if I were grav'd already;
When I have quench'd this wildfire
In Ercole's tame blood, I'll tell you. *Exit.*

ERCOLE.
You have judged today
A most confused practice, that takes end
In as bloody a trial; and we may observe
By these great persons, and their indirect
Proceedings, shadowed in a veil of state,
Mountains are deformed heaps, swell'd up aloft,
Vales wholesomer, though lower and trod on oft.

SANITONELLA.
Well, I will put up my papers
And send them to France for a precedent,
That they may not say yet, but for one strange
Law-suit, we come somewhat near them. *Exeunt.*

Explicit Actus Quartus.

[V.i] *Enter* Jolenta, *and* Angiolella *great-bellied.*

JOLENTA.
How dost thou, friend? Welcome; thou and I

638. *Knight-Marshal*] "an officer of the English royal households, who had judicial cognizance of transgressions . . . within a radius of twelve miles from the king's palace" (*OED*).

Were playfellows together, little children,
So small a while ago that I presume
We are neither of us wise yet.

ANGIOLELLA.
A most sad truth on my part.

JOLENTA.
Why do you pluck your veil over your face?

ANGIOLELLA.
If you will believe truth,
There's nought more terrible to a guilty heart
Than the eye of a respected friend.

JOLENTA.
Say, friend, are you quick with child?

ANGIOLELLA.
Too sure.

JOLENTA.
How could you know
First of your child, when you quicken'd?

ANGIOLELLA.
How could you know, friend?
'Tis reported you are in the same taking.

JOLENTA.
Ha, ha, ha! So 'tis given out;
But Ercole's coming to life again has shrunk
And made invisible my great belly; yes, faith,
My being with child was merely in supposition,
Not practice.

ANGIOLELLA. You are happy: what would I give
To be a maid again!

JOLENTA.
Would you? To what purpose?
I would never give great purchase for that thing
Is in danger every hour to be lost. Pray thee, laugh:
A boy or a girl for a wager?

6.] *this edn.;* Why . . . vaile/ Ouer . . . face? *Q.*
9. Than] *Dyce;* As *Q.*
13. First of your] *Dyce;* Of your first *Q.*

8–9.] almost verbatim from Sidney's *Arcadia* I (Lucas, *Works*, I, 86).
15. *taking*] plight.
23. *purchase*] payment.

ANGIOLELLA. What heaven please.

JOLENTA.
Nay, nay, will you venture
A chain of pearl with me whether?

ANGIOLELLA.
I'll lay nothing;
I have ventur'd too much for't already—my fame.
I make no question, sister, you have heard
Of the intended combat.

JOLENTA. O, what else?
I have a sweetheart in't against a brother.

ANGIOLELLA.
And I a dead friend, I fear. What good counsel
Can you minister unto me?

JOLENTA. Faith, only this:
Since there's no means i'th' world to hinder it,
Let thou and I, wench, get as far as we can
From the noise of it.

ANGIOLELLA. Whither?

JOLENTA.
No matter, any whither.

ANGIOLELLA.
Any whither, so you go not by sea:
I cannot abide rough water.

JOLENTA.
Not endure to be tumbled? Say no more, then,
We'll be land-soldiers for that trick; take heart,
Thy boy shall be born a brave Roman.

ANGIOLELLA.
O, you mean to go to Rome, then.

JOLENTA.
Within there!

Enter a servant.

Bear this letter

40. rough] *Q (corr.)*; salt *Q (uncorr.)*.
45. S.D.] *Dyce; at end of line in Q.*

---

30. *I . . . question*] I have no doubt.
41. *tumbled*] Jolenta is referring cynically to Angiolella's experiences with Romelio, too.
42. *trick*] clever expedient.

To the Lord Ercole. Now, wench, I am for thee
All the world over.

ANGIOLELLA.
I, like your shade, pursue you. *Exeunt.*

[V.ii] *Enter* Prospero *and* Sanitonella.

PROSPERO.
Well, I do not think but to see you as pretty a piece of law-flesh!

SANITONELLA.
In time I may. Marry, I am resolved to take a new way for't. You have lawyers take their clients' fees, and their backs are no sooner turn'd, but they call them fools, and laugh at them.

PROSPERO.
That's ill done of them.

SANITONELLA.
There's one thing, too, that has a vild abuse in't.

PROSPERO.
What's that?

SANITONELLA.
Marry, this: that no proctor in the term time be tolerated to go to the tavern above six times i'th' forenoon.

PROSPERO.
Why, man?

SANITONELLA.
O, sir, it makes their clients overtaken,
And become friends sooner than they would be.

Enter Ercole *with a letter, and* Contarino *coming in friars' habits, as having been at the Bathanites, a ceremony used afore these combats.*

3–4. In . . . for't] *Dyce;* In . . . may,/ Marry . . . for't *Q.*
10–11.] *Dyce;* Marry this/ That . . . forenoone *Q.*

46. *I am for thee*] equivalent of "I'm with you."
48. *shade*] shadow.
[V.ii]
10–11.] Sanitonella is speaking of his proposed reform rather than the abuse (Lucas).
13. *overtaken*] drunk.
14.2. *Bathanites*] Webster seems to have invented a ceremony, perhaps using a corrupted name of a religious order, either Bethlemites or Bethanites. Stoll suggests "Bataniti," a Moslem sect, which is inappropriate here.

ERCOLE.
Leave the room, gentlemen.
[*Exeunt* Sanitonella *and* Prospero.]

CONTARINO [*aside*].
Wherefore should I with such an obstinacy
Conceal myself any longer? I am taught
That all the blood which will be shed tomorrow
Must fall upon my head; one question
Shall fix it or untie it. [*To* Ercole.] Noble brother,
I would fain know how it is possible,
When it appears you love the fair Jolenta
With such a height of fervor, you were ready
To father another's child and marry her,
You would so suddenly engage yourself
To kill her brother, one that ever stood
Your loyal and firm friend?

ERCOLE. Sir, I'll tell you:
My love, as I have formerly protested,
To Contarino, whose unfortunate end
The traitor wrought; and here is one thing more
Deads all good thoughts of him, which I now receiv'd
From Jolenta.

CONTARINO.
In a letter?

ERCOLE. Yes, in this letter;
For, having sent to her to be resolved
Most truly, who was father of the child,
She writes back that the shame she goes withal
Was begot by her brother.

CONTARINO.
O most incestuous villain!

ERCOLE.
I protest, before, I thought 'twas Contarino's issue,
And for that would have veil'd her dishonor.

15.1] *Dyce.*
16. S.D.] *Dyce;* "Con. *speaks aside*" *at ll. 17–18 in Q.*
20. S.D.] *Lucas.*
38. incestuous] *Dyce;* incestious *Q.*

---

37. *begot*] called into being (*OED*); the ambiguity leads to the worst interpretation by Ercole and Contarino.

CONTARINO.
No more! Has the armorer brought the weapons?
ERCOLE.
Yes, sir.
CONTARINO. I will no more think of her.
ERCOLE.
Of whom?
CONTARINO.
Of my mother—I was thinking of my mother.
Call the armorer. *Exeunt.*

[V.iii] *Enter* Surgeon *and* Winifrid.

WINIFRID.
You do love me, sir, you say?
SURGEON.
O, most entirely!
WINIFRID. And you will marry me?
SURGEON.
Nay, I'll do more than that.
The fashion of the world is many times
To make a woman naught, and afterwards
To marry her; but I, o'th' contrary,
Will make you honest first, and afterwards
Proceed to the wedlock.
WINIFRID. Honest! What mean you by that?
SURGEON.
I mean, that your suborning the late law-suit
Has got you a filthy report: now there's no way,
But to do some excellent piece of honesty,
To recover your good name.
WINIFRID. How, sir?
SURGEON.
You shall straight go, and reveal to your old mistress
For certain truth, Contarino is alive.

41.] *this edn.;* No more./ Has . . . weapons? *Q.*

[V.iii]
13–14.] *Dyce;* You . . . old/ Mistris . . . aliue *Q.*

7,8. *honest*] Winifrid at first misunderstands the Surgeon to mean "chaste."

9. *suborning*] helping, with a sinister motive.

WINIFRID.
How, living?
SURGEON. Yes, he is living.
WINIFRID.
No, I must not tell her of it.
SURGEON. No! Why?
WINIFRID.
For she did bind me yesterday, by oath,
Never more to speak of him.
SURGEON.
You shall reveal it, then, to Ariosto the judge.
WINIFRID.
By no means; he has heard me tell
So many lies i'th' court, he'll ne'er believe me.
What if I told it to the Capuchin?
SURGEON. You cannot
Think of a better; as for your young mistress,
Who, as you told me, has persuaded you
To run away with her—let her have her humor.
I have a suit Romelio left i'th' house,
The habit of a Jew, that I'll put on,
And pretending I am robb'd, by break of day,
Procure all passengers to be brought back,
And by the way reveal myself, and discover
The comical event. They say she's a little mad;
This will help to cure her. Go, go presently,
And reveal it to the Capuchin.
WINIFRID. Sir, I shall. *Exeunt.*

[V.iv] *Enter* Julio, Prospero, *and* Sanitonella.

JULIO.
A pox on't, I have undertaken the challenge very foolishly: what if I do not appear to answer it?

20–21.] *Dyce;* By . . . me/ Tell . . . mee *Q.*
22–23. You . . . mistress] *Dyce; one line in Q.*
23. as for] *Dyce;* for as *Q.*
23. mistress] *Dyce;* M^ris *Q.*

15. *How*] what; short for "how say you?"
29. *Procure*] cause.

PROSPERO.

It would be absolute conviction
Of cowardice and perjury; and the Dane
May, to your public shame, reverse your arms,
Or have them ignominiously fasten'd
Under his horse-tail.

JULIO.

I do not like that so well.
I see, then, I must fight, whether I will or no.

PROSPERO.

How does Romelio bear himself? They say
He has almost brain'd one of our cunning'st fencers
That practic'd with him.

JULIO.

Very certain; and, now you talk of fencing,
Do not you remember the Welsh gentleman
That was traveling to Rome upon return?

PROSPERO.

No, what of him?

JULIO.

There was a strange experiment of a fencer.

PROSPERO.

What was that?

JULIO.

The Welshman in's play, do what the fencer could,
Hung still an arse—he could not for's life
Make him come on bravely—till, one night at supper,
Observing what a deal of Parma cheese
His scholar devoured, goes ingeniously
The next morning and makes a spacious button
For his foil of toasted cheese; and, as sure as you live,
That made him come on the braveliest.

6. ignominiously] *Dyce*; ignomiously *Q*.

4. *Dane*] Contarino, still disguised.

5. *reverse your arms*] turn your coat of arms upside down.

15. *upon return*] traveling in hopes of making money by having people at home wager heavily against his safe return (Lucas).

20. *Hung still an arse*] continued to hang back.

22. *Parma cheese*] Parmesan cheese; the Welsh love of cheese was proverbial.

PROSPERO. Possible?

JULIO.
Marry, it taught him an ill grace in's play,
It made him gape still, gape as he put in for't,
As I have seen some hungry usher.

SANITONELLA.
The toasting of it belike
Was to make it more supple, had he chanc'd
To have hit him o'th' chaps.

JULIO.
Not unlikely. Who can tell me
If we may breathe in the duel?

PROSPERO. By no means.

JULIO.
Nor drink?

PROSPERO.
Neither.

JULIO.
That's scurvy; anger will make me very dry.

PROSPERO.
You mistake, sir; 'tis sorrow that is very dry.

SANITONELLA.
Not always, sir; I have known sorrow very wet.

JULIO.
In rainy weather?

SANITONELLA.
No, when a woman has come dropping wet
Out of a cucking-stool.

JULIO.
Then 'twas wet indeed, sir.

Enter Romelio *very melancholy, and the* Capuchin.

---

28. *put in*] made a thrust.

32. *chaps*] the jaws or lower cheeks.

34. *breathe*] pause for breath.

37–38. *anger . . . sorrow . . . dry*] Choler was considered hot and dry; black bile or melancholy was cold and dry.

42. *cucking-stool*] a seat at the end of a pole to which scolds and other offenders were fastened and ducked into water.

CAPUCHIN [*aside*].

Having from Leonora's waiting-woman
Deliver'd a most strange intelligence
Of Contarino's recovery, I am come
To sound Romelio's penitence; that perform'd,
To end these errors by discovering
What she related to me. —[*To* Romelio.] Peace to you, sir.
Pray, gentlemen, let the freedom of this room
Be mine a little —[*To* Julio.] Nay, sir, you may stay.

Exeunt Prospero, Sanitonella.

Will you pray with me?

ROMELIO.

No, no, the world and I
Have not made up our accounts yet.

CAPUCHIN.

Shall I pray for you?

ROMELIO.

Whether you do or no, I care not.

CAPUCHIN.

O, you have a dangerous voyage to take.

ROMELIO.

No matter, I will be mine own pilot:
Do not you trouble your head with the business.

CAPUCHIN.

Pray tell me, do not you meditate of death?

ROMELIO.

Phew, I took out that lesson
When I once lay sick of an ague; I do now
Labor for life, for life! Sir, can you tell me
Whether your Toledo or your Milan blade
Be best temper'd?

CAPUCHIN.

These things, you know, are out of my practice.

44. S.D.] *Dyce.*
49. S.D.] *Dyce.*
51. S.D. *To* Julio] *Dyce.*

---

64. *Toledo . . . Milan blade*] Toledo, Spain, was famous for its swords; Milan was known for a wider range of armor.
66. *practice*] customary scope of action.

ROMELIO.

But these are things, you know,
I must practice with tomorrow.

CAPUCHIN.

Were I in your case,
I should present to myself strange shadows.

ROMELIO.

Turn you, were I in your case,
I should laugh at mine own shadow.
Who has hired you to make me coward?

CAPUCHIN.

I would make you a good Christian.

ROMELIO.

Withal let me continue
An honest man, which I am very certain
A coward can never be. You take upon you
A physician's place, rather than a divine's.
You go about to bring my body so low,
I should fight i'th' lists tomorrow like a dormouse,
And be made away in a slumber.

CAPUCHIN.

Did you murder Contarino?

ROMELIO.

That's a scurvy question now.

CAPUCHIN. Why, sir?

ROMELIO.

Did you ask it as a confessor, or as a spy?

CAPUCHIN.

As one that fain would justle the devil
Out of your way.

72. own] *Dyce;* one *Q*.

---

69. *case*] plight.
70. *shadows*] foreshadowings, premonitions.
71. *Turn you*] look at it from another angle.
71. *case*] clothing. Romelio can now move on to a second pun, on *shadow*.
81. *slumber*] a bit of word play growing from the first syllable of "dormouse," *dormire*, French for "sleep."
85. *justle*] jostle.

ROMELIO.

Um, you are but weakly made for't.
He's a cunning wrestler, I can tell you,
And has broke many a man's neck.

CAPUCHIN.

But to give him the foil goes not by strength.

ROMELIO.

Let it go by what it will.
Get me some good victuals to breakfast—I am hungry.

CAPUCHIN.

Here's food for you. *Offering him a book.*

ROMELIO.

Phew, I am not to commence doctor;
For then the word, "Devour that book," were proper.
I am to fight, to fight, sir, and I'll do't
As I would feed, with a good stomach.

CAPUCHIN.

Can you feed, and apprehend death?

ROMELIO.

Why, sir, is not death
A hungry companion? Say, is not the grave
Said to be a great devourer? Get me some victuals.
I knew a man that was to lose his head
Feed with an excellent good appetite,
To strengthen his heart, scarce half an hour before.
And if he did it, that only was to speak,
What should I, that am to do?

CAPUCHIN.

This confidence,
If it be grounded upon truth, 'tis well.

ROMELIO.

You must understand that resolution

88–89.] *this edn.; prose in Q.*

---

90. *foil*] a throw in wrestling.
94. *commence doctor*] begin study for a doctorate.
95. *word*] motto (Dyce).
98. *apprehend*] understand the meaning of.
105. *speak*] say last words before execution.
106. *What . . . do*] Romelio needs even more strength, for he must be physically active.

Should ever wait upon a noble death,
As captains bring their soldiers out o'th' field
And come off last. For, I pray, what is death?
The safest trench i'th' world to keep man free
From Fortune's gunshot; to be afraid of that
Would prove me weaker than a teeming woman,
That does endure a thousand times more pain
In bearing of a child.

CAPUCHIN.

O, I tremble for you!
For I do know you have a storm within you
More terrible than a sea fight, and your soul
Being heretofore drown'd in security,
You know not how to live, nor how to die.
But I have an object that shall startle you,
And make you know whither you are going.

ROMELIO.

I am arm'd for't.

Enter Leonora, *with two coffins borne by her servants, and two winding-sheets stuck with flowers; presents one to her son, and the other to* Julio.

'Tis very welcome; this is a decent garment
Will never be out of fashion. I will kiss it.
All the flowers of the spring
Meet to perfume our burying:
These have but their growing prime,
And man does flourish but his time.
Survey our progress from our birth:
We are set, we grow, we turn to earth.
Courts adieu, and all delights, *Soft music.*
All bewitching appetites;
Sweetest breath, and clearest eye,
Like perfumes, go out and die;
And consequently this is done,
As shadows wait upon the sun.
Vain the ambition of kings,
Who seek by trophies and dead things
To leave a living name behind,
And weave but nets to catch the wind.

---

110. *wait upon*] be attendant upon.
115. *teeming*] childbearing.

O, you have wrought a miracle, and melted
A heart of adamant; you have compris'd,
In this dumb pageant, a right excellent form
Of penitence.

CAPUCHIN. I am glad you so receive it.

ROMELIO.
This object does persuade me to forgive
The wrong she has done me, which I count the way
To be forgiven yonder; and this shroud
Shows me how rankly we do smell of earth,
When we are in all our glory. Will it please you *To his mother.*
Enter that closet, where I shall confer
'Bout matters of most weighty consequence,
Before the duel? *Exit* Leonora [*into the closet*].

JULIO [*draping the shroud over his shoulder*].
Now I am right in the bandoleer for th' gallows.
What a scurvy fashion 'tis, to hang
One's coffin in a scarf!

CAPUCHIN. Why, this is well:
And now that I have made you fit for death,
And brought you even as low as is the grave,
I will raise you up again, speak comforts to you
Beyond your hopes, turn this intended duel
To a triumph.

ROMELIO. More divinity yet?
Good sir, do one thing first: there's in my closet
A prayer book that is cover'd with gilt vellum—
Fetch it, and pray you certify my mother,
I'll presently come to her.
Exit Capuchin *after* Leonora. Romelio] *locks him into a closet.*
So, now you are safe.

152. S.D.] *Hazlitt; at ll. 148–149 in Q.*
155. S.D. *into the closet*] *Dyce.*
157–158. What . . . scarf] *this edn.; one line in Q.*
167. S.D.] *Dyce; "locks him into a closet" at end of line in Q.*

---

150. *yonder*] in the afterlife.
156. *bandoleer*] broad sash or belt worn over the shoulder and across the chest.
166. *certify*] assure.
167,169. *safe*] unable to escape or intervene.

JULIO.
What have you done?

ROMELIO. Why, I have lock'd them up
Into a turret of the castle, safe enough
For troubling us this four hours; and he please,
He may open a casement, and whistle out to th' sea
Like a boatswain; not any creature can hear him.
Wast not thou a-weary of his preaching?

JULIO.
Yes, if he had had an hourglass by him,
I would have wish'd him he would have jogg'd it a little.
But your mother, your mother's lock'd in too.

ROMELIO.
So much the better;
I am rid of her howling at parting.

JULIO.
Hark! He knocks to be let out, and he were mad.

ROMELIO.
Let him knock till his sandals fly in pieces.

JULIO.
Ha! What says he? Contarino living?

ROMELIO.
Ay, ay, he means he would have Contarino's living
Bestowed upon his monastery; 'tis that
He only fishes for. So, 'tis break of day;
We shall be call'd to the combat presently.

JULIO.
I am sorry for one thing.

ROMELIO. What's that?

JULIO.
That I made not mine own ballad: I do fear
I shall be roguishly abused in meter
If I miscarry. Well, if the young Capuchin
Do not talk o'th' flesh as fast now to your mother
As he did to us o'th' spirit! If he do,

---

179. *and*] as though.
182. *living*] estates and possessions.
183–184. *that . . . for*] that alone that he fishes for.

'Tis not the first time that the prison royal
Has been guilty of close committing.

ROMELIO.
Now to th' combat. [*Exeunt*].

[V.v] *Enter* Capuchin *and* Leonora *above at a window.*

LEONORA.
Contarino living?

CAPUCHIN.
Yes, madam, he is living, and Ercole's second.

LEONORA.
Why has he lock'd us up thus?

CAPUCHIN. Some evil angel
Makes him deaf to his own safety. We are shut
Into a turret, the most desolate prison
Of all the castle; and his obstinacy,
Madness, or secret fate has thus prevented
The saving of his life.

LEONORA.
O, the saving Contarino's!
His is worth nothing. For heaven's sake call louder.

CAPUCHIN.
To little purpose.

LEONORA.
I will leap these battlements;
And may I be found dead time enough
To hinder the combat!

CAPUCHIN. O, look upwards rather:
Their deliverance must come thence. To see how heaven
Can invert man's firmest purpose! His intent
Of murdering Contarino was a mean
To work his safety, and my coming hither
To save him is his ruin. Wretches turn
The tide of their good fortune, and being drench'd
In some presumptuous and hidden sins,

194. S.D.] *Dyce.*

193. *close committing*] committing adultery, with a hint of the second meaning, "imprisonment."

While they aspire to do themselves most right,
The devil that rules i'th'air hangs in their light.

LEONORA.
O, they must not be lost thus! Some good Christian
Come within our hearing! Ope the other casement
That looks into the city.

CAPUCHIN. Madam, I shall. *Exeunt.*

[V.vi]

The lists set up. Enter the Marshal, Crispiano, *and* Ariosto, *as Judges; they sit.* [*With them,* Sanitonella, *attendants, and* Herald.]

MARSHAL.
Give the appellant his summons; do the like
To the defendant.

Two tuckets by several trumpets. Enter at one door, Ercole *and* Contarino; *at the other,* Romelio *and* Julio.

Can any of you allege aught why the combat
Should not proceed?

COMBATANTS. Nothing

ARIOSTO. Have the knights weighed
And measured their weapons?

MARSHAL. They have.

ARIOSTO.
Proceed, then, to the battle, and may heaven
Determine the right!

HERALD.
Soit la battaile, et victoire à ceux qui ont droit!

ROMELIO.
Stay, I do not well know whither I am going;
'Twere needful therefore, though at the last gasp,
To have some churchman's prayer. Run, I pray thee,
To Castel Novo; this key will release

24–26. O . . . city] *Dyce; prose in Q.*
[V.vi]
0.2. *With* them Sanitonella] *Lucas*
0.2. *attendants, and* Herald] *this edn.*
8,15,16. *victoire . . . droit*] *Dyce; Victory a ceux que droit Q.*

2.1. *tuckets*] individualized signals to summon the combatants; noblemen often had their own trumpet calls.

12. *Castel Novo*] Castel Nuovo, Anjevin and Spanish-built fortress on a small point overlooking the Bay of Naples.

A Capuchin and my mother, whom I shut
Into a turret. Bid them make haste, and pray;
I may be dead ere he comes. [*Exit an attendant.*]
Now, *victoire, à ceux qui ont droit!*

ALL THE CHAMP.
Victoire à ceux qui ont droit!

The combat continued to a good length, when enters Leonora *and the* Capuchin.

LEONORA.
Hold, hold, for heaven's sake, hold!

ARIOSTO.
What are these that interrupt the combat?
Away to prison with them.

CAPUCHIN.
We have been prisoners too long.
O, sir, what mean you? Contarino's living.

ERCOLE.
Living!

CAPUCHIN. Behold him living.

[Contarino *removes disguise.*]

ERCOLE.
You were but now my second; now I make you
Myself forever.

LEONORA. O, here's one between,
Claims to be nearer.

CONTARINO. And to you, dear lady,
I have entirely vowed my life.

ROMELIO.
If I do not dream, I am happy too.

ARIOSTO.
How insolently has this high Court of Honor
Been abused!

Enter Angiolella *veil'd and* Jolenta, *her face color'd like a Moor; the two Surgeons, one of them like a Jew.*

How now, who are these?

15. S.D.] *Dyce.*

16. S.P. *Champ*] the "field," presumably the combatants and the various attendants.

SECOND SURGEON.

A couple of strange fowl, and I the falconer
That have sprung them. This is a white nun
Of the order of Saint Clare; and this a black one,
You'll take my word for't. *Discovers* Jolenta.

ARIOSTO. She's a black one, indeed.

JOLENTA.

Like or dislike me, choose you whether:
The down upon the raven's feather
Is as gentle and as sleek
As the mole on Venus' cheek.
Hence, vain show! I only care
To preserve my soul most fair;
Never mind the outward skin,
But the jewel that's within;
And though I want the crimson blood,
Angels boast my sisterhood.
Which of us now judge you whiter,
Her whose credit proves the lighter,
Or this black and ebon hue,
That, unstain'd, keeps fresh and true?
For I proclaim't without control,
There's no true beauty but i'th' soul.

ERCOLE.

O, tis the fair Jolenta! To what purpose
Are you thus eclips'd?

JOLENTA.

Sir, I was running away
From the rumor of this combat; I fled likewise
From the untrue report my brother spread,
To his politic ends, that I was got with child.

LEONORA.

Cease here all further scrutiny; this paper
Shall give unto the court each circumstance
Of all these passages.

ARIOSTO.

No more! Attend the sentence of the court.

---

31. *sprung*] caused to rise from cover.
42. *crimson blood*] Blood shows as pink cheeks in Caucasians.

Rareness and difficulty give estimation
To all things are i'th' world: you have met both
In these several passages; now it does remain
That these so comical events be blasted
With no severity of sentence. You, Romelio,
Shall first deliver to that gentleman,
Who stood your second, all those obligations
Wherein he stands engaged to you, receiving
Only the principal.

ROMELIO. I shall, my lord.

JULIO.

I thank you.
I have an humor now to go to sea
Against the pirates; and my only ambition
Is to have my ship furnish'd with a rare consort
Of music; and when I am pleased to be mad,
They shall play me *Orlando*.

SANITONELLA.

You must lay wait for the fiddlers;
They'll fly away from the press like watermen.

ARIOSTO.

Next, you shall marry that nun.

ROMELIO. Most willingly.

ANGIOLELLA.

O sir, you have been unkind;
But I do only wish that this my shame
May warn all honest virgins not to seek
The way to heaven, that is so wondrous steep,
Through those vows they are too frail to keep.

ARIOSTO.

Contarino, and Romelio, and yourself,

67–68. Wherein . . . principal] *Dyce;* Wherein . . . you,/ Receiuing . . . principall *Q*.

---

60. *give estimation*] give added reputation.

63. *comical*] fortunate in their outcome.

72–73. *consort/ Of music*] small company of musicians.

74. *Orlando*] *Orlando Furioso*, probably Robert Greene's romance based vaguely on Ariosto.

76. *fly . . . press*] watermen with a knowledge of boat handling sought ways to escape being impressed into the navy.

Shall for seven years maintain against the Turk
Six galleys. Leonora, Jolenta,
And Angiolella there, the beauteous nun,
For their vows' breach unto the monastery,
Shall build a monastery. Lastly, the two surgeons,
For concealing Contarino's recovery,
Shall exercise their art at their own charge
For a twelvemonth in the galleys. So we leave you,
Wishing your future life may make good use
Of these events, since that these passages,
Which threaten'd ruin, built on rotten ground,
Are with success beyond our wishes crown'd. *Exeunt omnes.*

FINIS.

93. *passages*] things coming to pass.

Appendix

Chronology

Approximate years are indicated by *, occurrences in doubt by (?).

Political and Literary Events	*Life and Major Works of Webster*
1558 Accession of Queen Elizabeth I. Robert Greene born. Thomas Kyd born.	
1560 George Chapman born.	
1561 Francis Bacon born.	
1564 Shakespeare born. Christopher Marlowe born.	
1572 Thomas Dekker born.* John Donne born. Massacre of St. Bartholomew's Day.	
1573 Ben Jonson born.*	
1574 Thomas Heywood born.*	
1576 The Theatre, the first permanent public theater in London, established by James Burbage. John Marston born.	
1577 The Curtain theater opened. Holinshed's *Chronicles of England, Scotland and Ireland.*	

Drake begins circumnavigation of the earth; completed 1580.

1578
John Lyly's *Euphues: The Anatomy of Wit.*

1579
John Fletcher born.
Sir Thomas North's translation of Plutarch's *Lives.*

1580
Thomas Middleton born. John Webster born.*

1583
Philip Massinger born.

1584
Francis Beaumont born.*

1586
Death of Sir Philip Sidney.
John Ford born.
Kyd's *THE SPANISH TRAGEDY.**

1587
The Rose theater opened by Henslowe.
Marlowe's *TAMBURLAINE,* Part I.*
Execution of Mary, Queen of Scots.
Drake raids Cadiz.

1588
Defeat of the Spanish Armada.
Marlowe's *TAMBURLAINE,* Part II.*

1589
Greene's *FRIAR BACON AND FRIAR BUNGAY.**
Marlowe's *THE JEW OF MALTA.**

1590
Spenser's *Faerie Queene* (Books I–III) published.
Sidney's *Arcadia* published.
Shakespeare's *HENRY VI,* Parts I–III,* *TITUS ANDRONICUS.**

1591
Shakespeare's RICHARD III.*

1592
Marlowe's *DOCTOR FAUSTUS** and *EDWARD II.**
Shakespeare's *TAMING OF THE SHREW** and *THE COMEDY OF ERRORS.**
Death of Greene.

1593
Shakespeare's *LOVE'S LABOR'S LOST:** *Venus and Adonis* published.
Death of Marlowe.
Theaters closed on account of plague.

1594
Shakespeare's *TWO GENTLEMEN OF VERONA;** *The Rape of Lucrece* published.
Shakespeare's company becomes Lord Chamberlain's Men.
Death of Kyd.

1595
The Swan theater built.
Sidney's *Defense of Poesy* published.
Shakespeare's *ROMEO AND JULIET,** *A MIDSUMMER NIGHT'S DREAM.**
*RICHARD II.**
Raleigh's first expedition to Guiana.

1596
Spenser's *Faerie Queene* (Books IV–VI) published.
Shakespeare's *MERCHANT OF VENICE,** *KING JOHN.**
James Shirley born.

1597
Bacon's *Essays* (first edition).
Shakespeare's *HENRY IV*, Part I.*

1598
Demolition of The Theatre. | Admitted to Middle Temple (?).

Shakespeare's *MUCH ADO ABOUT NOTHING,** *HENRY IV,* Part II.*
Jonson's *EVERY MAN IN HIS HUMOR* (first version).
Seven books of Chapman's translation of Homer's *Iliad* published.

1599
The Paul's Boys reopen their theater.
The Globe theater opened.
Shakespeare's *AS YOU LIKE IT,** *HENRY V, JULIUS CAESAR.**
Marston's *ANTONIO AND MELLIDA,** Parts I and II.
Dekker's *THE SHOEMAKERS' HOLIDAY.**
Death of Spenser.

1600
Shakespeare's *TWELFTH NIGHT.**
The Fortune theater built by Alleyn.
The Children of the Chapel begin to play at the Blackfriars.

Collaborates on *THE WEAKEST GOETH TO THE WALL* (?).

1601
Shakespeare's *HAMLET,** *MERRY WIVES OF WINDSOR.**
Insurrection and execution of the Earl of Essex.
Jonson's *POETASTER.*

1602
Shakespeare's *TROILUS AND CRESSIDA.**

Henslowe pays for his share in *CAESAR'S FALL* (= *TWO SHAPES*?) (lost), Part I of *LADY JANE* (= *SIR THOMAS WYATT*?), *CHRISTMAS COMES BUT ONCE A YEAR* (lost).
Occasional verses for Munday's *Palmerin of England,* Part III.

1603
Death of Queen Elizabeth I;

accession of James VI of Scotland as James I.
Florio's translation of Montaigne's *Essays* published.
Shakespeare's *ALL'S WELL THAT ENDS WELL.**
Heywood's *A WOMAN KILLED WITH KINDNESS.*
Marston's *THE MALCONTENT.**
Shakespeare's company becomes the King's Men.

1604
Shakespeare's *MEASURE FOR MEASURE,* OTHELLO.**
Marston's *THE FAWN.**
Chapman's *BUSSY D'AMBOIS.**

Collaborates with Dekker on *WESTWARD HO!** (registered, 1605; printed, 1607).
Induction to Marston's *MALCONTENT*; occasional Ode for Harrison's *Arches of Triumph.*

1605
Shakespeare's *KING LEAR.**
Marston's *THE DUTCH COURTESAN.**
Bacon's *Advancement of Learning* published.
The Gunpowder Plot.

Collaborates with Dekker on *NORTHWARD HO!** (printed, 1607).

1606
Shakespeare's *MACBETH.**
Jonson's *VOLPONE.**
Tourneur's *REVENGER'S TRAGEDY.**
The Red Bull theater built.
Death of John Lyly.

1607
Shakespeare's *ANTONY AND CLEOPATRA.**
Beaumont's *KNIGHT OF THE BURNING PESTLE.**
Settlement of Jamestown, Virginia.

THE FAMOUS HISTORIE OF SIR THOMAS WYATT printed with title-page attribution to Dekker and Webster (= *LADY JANE*?).

1608
Shakespeare's *CORIOLANUS, TIMON OF ATHENS,* PERICLES.**

Chapman's *CONSPIRACY AND TRAGEDY OF CHARLES, DUKE OF BYRON.**
Richard Burbage leases Blackfriars theater for King's company.
John Milton born.

1609
Shakespeare's *CYMBELINE*;*
Sonnets published.
Jonson's *EPICOENE.*
Dekker's *Gull's Hornbook* published.

Daughter Alice baptized at St. Leonard's (?).

1610
Jonson's *ALCHEMIST.*
Chapman's *REVENGE OF BUSSY D'AMBOIS.**
Richard Crashaw born.

1611
Authorized (King James) Version of the Bible published.
Shakespeare's *THE WINTER'S TALE,* THE TEMPEST.**
Beaumont's and Fletcher's *A KING AND NO KING.*
Middleton's *A CHASTE MAID IN CHEAPSIDE.**
Tourneur's *ATHEIST'S TRAGEDY.**
Chapman's translation of *Iliad* completed.

*THE WHITE DEVIL** (printed, 1612, 1631).

1612

A Monumental Column, Erected to the Living Memory of the ever-glorious Henry, late Prince of Wales, in Three Eligies on the most lamented death of Prince Henry (printed, 1613).
Occasional verses for Heywood's *Apology for Actors.*

1613
The Globe theater burned.
Shakespeare's *HENRY VIII* (with Fletcher).
Sir Thomas Overbury murdered.

*THE DUCHESS OF MALFI** (printed, 1623).

1614	
The Globe theater rebuilt. The Hope theater built. Jonson's *BARTHOLOMEW FAIR.*	*THE GUISE** (lost; written sometime before 1623).
1615	
	Contributes thirty-two "New Characters" to sixth edition of Overbury's *Characters* (?).
1616	
Publication of Folio edition of Jonson's *Works.* Chapman's *Whole Works of Homer.* Death of Shakespeare. Death of Beaumont.	
1617	
	DUCHESS OF MALFI revised and revived.*
1618	
Outbreak of Thirty Years War. Execution of Raleigh.	
1619	
	*THE DEVIL'S LAW-CASE** (printed, 1623).
1620	
Settlement of Plymouth, Massachusetts.	
1621	
Middleton's *WOMEN BEWARE WOMEN.** Robert Burton's *Anatomy of Melancholy* published. Andrew Marvell born.	Collaborates with Middleton on *ANYTHING FOR A QUIET LIFE* (?).
1622	
Middleton and Rowley's *THE CHANGELING.** Henry Vaughan born.	
1623	
Publication of Folio edition of Shakespeare's *COMEDIES, HISTORIES, AND TRAGEDIES.*	Occasional verses for Cockeram's *English Dictionarie.*

1624

Collaborates with Ford, Dekker, and Rowley on *THE LATE MURDER OF THE SON UPON THE MOTHER*, or *KEEP THE WIDOW WAKING* (licensed, September; lost).
The Lord Mayor's Pageant, *MONUMENTS OF HONOUR* (performed, October 29).
Verses on an engraved portrait of the family of James I (?).

1625

Death of King James I; accession of Charles I.
Death of Fletcher.

Collaborates with Rowley (and Heywood?) on *A CURE FOR A CUCKOLD** (printed, 1661).
Collaborates with Fletcher, Massinger, and Ford on *THE FAIR MAID OF THE INN* (?) (licensed to Fletcher, 1626; printed in the Beaumont and Fletcher Folio of 1647).

1626

Death of Tourneur.
Death of Bacon.

Collaborates with Heywood on *APPIUS AND VIRGINIA* (?) (printed 1654, may date back to 1603).

1627

Death of Middleton.

1628

Ford's *THE LOVER'S MELANCHOLY.*
Petition of Right.
Buckingham assassinated.

1630

DUCHESS OF MALFI given a Court performance by the King's Men at the Cockpit, December 26.

1631

Shirley's *THE TRAITOR.*
Death of Donne.
John Dryden born.

1632

Massinger's *THE CITY MADAM.**

1633

Donne's *Poems* published.
Death of George Herbert.

1634

Death of Chapman, Marston.
Publication of *THE TWO NOBLE KINSMEN*, with title-page attribution to Shakespeare and Fletcher.
Milton's *Comus*.

Death of Webster.*

1635

Sir Thomas Browne's *Religio Medici*.

1637

Death of Jonson.

1639

First Bishops' War.
Death of Carew.*

1640

Short Parliament.
Long Parliament impeaches Laud.
Death of Massinger, Burton.

1641

Irish rebel.
Death of Heywood.

1642

Charles I leaves London; Civil War breaks out.
Shirley's *COURT SECRET*.
All theaters closed by Act of Parliament.

1643

Parliament swears to the Solemn League and Covenant.

1645

Ordinance for New Model Army enacted.

1646

End of First Civil War.

1647

Army occupies London.
Charles I forms alliance with Scots.
Publication of Folio edition of

Beaumont and Fletcher's *COMEDIES AND TRAGEDIES.*

1648

Second Civil War.

1649

Execution of Charles I.

1650

Jeremy Collier born.

1651

Hobbes' *Leviathan* published.

1652

First Dutch War began (ended 1654).

Thomas Otway born.

1653

Nathaniel Lee born.*

1656

D'Avenant's *THE SIEGE OF RHODES* performed at Rutland House.

1657

John Dennis born.

1658

Death of Oliver Cromwell.

D'Avenant's *THE CRUELTY OF THE SPANIARDS IN PERU* performed at the Cockpit.

1660

Restoration of Charles II.

Theatrical patents granted to Thomas Killigrew and Sir William D'Avenant, authorizing them to form, respectively, the King's and the Duke of York's Companies.

1661

Cowley's *THE CUTTER OF COLEMAN STREET.*

D'Avenant's *THE SIEGE OF RHODES* (expanded to two parts).

1662

Charter granted to the Royal Society.

1663
Dryden's *THE WILD GALLANT.*
Tuke's *THE ADVENTURES OF FIVE HOURS.*

1664
Sir John Vanbrugh born.
Dryden's *THE RIVAL LADIES.*
Dryden and Howard's *THE INDIAN QUEEN.*
Etherege's *THE COMICAL REVENGE.*

1665
Second Dutch War began (ended 1667).
Great Plague.
Dryden's *THE INDIAN EMPEROR.*
Orrery's *MUSTAPHA.*

1666
Fire of London.
Death of James Shirley.